ALFA ROMEO

HAYNES CLASSIC MAKES SERIES

ALFA ROMEO

ALWAYS WITH PASSION

Second edition

DAVID OWEN

First edition published in August 1999
Second edition published in October 2004

British Library Cataloguing in Publication Data:
A catalogue record for this book is available from the British Library

ISBN 1 84425 117 9

Library of Congress control no. 2004106167

Published by Haynes Publishing, Sparkford, Yeovil, Somerset BA22 7JJ, UK
Tel: 01963 442030 Fax: 01963 440001
Int. tel: +44 1963 442030 Fax: +44 1963 440001
E-mail: sales@haynes.co.uk
Web site: www.haynes.co.uk

Haynes North America, Inc.
861 Lawrence Drive, Newbury Park,
California 91320, USA

Printed and bound in Great Britain by J. H. Haynes & Co. Ltd, Sparkford

contents

Alfa Romeo
introduction

Some car marques have more colourful histories than others, and Alfa Romeo must deserve a place very close to the top of the list in this respect. This is a company that, at several times in its long history, has come very close indeed to disaster. The lot of a maker of thoroughbred quality cars has never been an easy one, but on several occasions the company found itself producing a limited range of large, expensive and opulent machines, which had cost a lot of time, effort and hard cash to develop, at the very moment when the bottom dropped out of the market. Crippled by the First World War, wrong-footed by the Wall Street Crash, and heavily bombed in the Second World War, Alfa Romeo should have disappeared into the history books decades ago. But had it done so, the car world would have been an infinitely poorer place for its passing.

Now Alfa Romeo's place in motoring history is at least secure, with a long and splendid tradition of classic designs. Yet it wasn't always so. The company began in 1906 under the name of SAID, Societa Anonima

The first Alfa model, Merosi's massively imposing 24HP Torpedo of 1910.
(Alfa Romeo archives)

Vettura da corsa A.L.F.A tipo Grand Prix 1914
— Cilindrata litri 4,500 - Km lanciato in 24"⅘ (Km 148 all'ora) —   8973

Alfa's first designer, Giuseppe Merosi, sitting at the wheel of his most ambitious creation, the 1914 A.L.F.A. Grand Prix car, with his colleague, Ing. Faragiana. (Alfa Romeo archives)

Italiana Darracq, turning out cars that were totally unsuited to local conditions, unreliable and underpowered, and dumped on the Italian market in an attempt to increase the fortune of the French entrepreneur Alexandre Darracq.

Fortunately, such a catastrophic miscalculation brought swift commercial retribution. Within three years the company was on the verge of bankruptcy, and was reconstituted under a different set of initials, changing its name from SAID to Anonima Lombarda Fabbrica Automobili, or A.L.F.A. Fortunately for its future, the cars changed too. A former building surveyor turned car designer, Giuseppe Merosi, was hired to produce a series of solid, reliable and relatively powerful machines, which began with the 24HP A.L.F.A. in 1910.

Although this big four-seater weighed more than a ton, with a leisurely 4-litre engine pushing it to a quoted

top speed of 62mph (100kph) it had considerably more performance than the Darracqs it replaced. Merosi then produced a slightly smaller and slightly lighter 2413cc version of the design, called the 15HP, equipped with a three-speed gearbox, and which could just manage a 55mph (90kph) top speed.

Neither of these machines set the Tiber on fire in terms of sporting qualities, but they proved popular enough with Italian buyers to rescue the company from liquidation. Furthermore, they stood up to the worst Italian roads of the time, which was a lot to ask any car. The other advantages of Merosi's conservative engine designs were that stresses were low, and there was plenty of room for improvement. As engine improvements delivered more power, performance began to improve, and the A.L.F.A. board could see that this was extremely popular with the customers.

For 1911 the company considered boosting its sporting image by one of two expedients. Either it produced a totally new high-performance design that would establish A.L.F.A. as a sports car producer beyond all question, or it could go motor racing.

In the event, it went for the racing option, but did it, as A.L.F.A. did everything else at this stage in its history, slowly and carefully.

Building a racing car in those early days was a relatively simple process. You cut the weight of the car as much as possible, by stripping away bodywork, seats, wings and anything else that could be spared. Then you applied some mild improvements to the engine, to raise the power output without compromising reliability. Just how modest the improvements were can be seen from the figures. The racing 24HP Corsa looked very different, with just a bare chassis aft of the dashboard, and a pair of bucket seats for the driver and mechanic. With narrower axles borrowed from the 15HP, weight was cut by one-eighth, to 17.25cwt (875kg), and the top speed climbed to a scarcely staggering 70mph (113kph).

Two of the cars were given perhaps the toughest challenge possible – the 1911 Targa Florio, 276 miles (444km) of epic racing over the rough mountain roads of Northern Sicily. The race was run in a downpour of tropical intensity and neither car finished. In 1912 the Targa was run as a 651-mile (1048km) circuit of the entire island, and the lone A.L.F.A. entered failed to finish that event too. But this small, tentative and initially unsuccessful step into the world of motor racing had started a process that would help to determine the course of the company's future history.

By 1913 Merosi had produced the 40-60HP, a bigger and more powerful A.L.F.A. with a massive 6082cc four-cylinder engine, fitted for the first time with much more efficient overhead valves. This delivered 73bhp, compared with the 42bhp of the original 24hp, although the weight increased too, to 24.6cwt (1250kg). Nevertheless, when stripped for racing, as the 40-60HP Corsa, the car

The huge but fast and completely dependable Alfa 40-60, seen here at the 1913 Parma to Poggio di Berceto hillclimb where it finished second overall, with company test driver Nino Franchini. (Alfa Romeo archives)

was capable of a top speed of 85mph (137kph), and could keep that speed up, if needed, for the several hours of a major motor race.

From the beginning, the 40-60 Corsa was a winner. On their very first outing, two cars finished first and second in their class in the Parma to Poggio di Berceto hillclimb, and the leader put up second fastest time overall. In May 1914, two cars were entered in the Coppa Florio, a shorter version of the Targa run over the same mountain course, where they finished third and fourth overall.

This was enough to persuade the directors to go the rest of the way, and commission Merosi to design a full-blooded Grand Prix car. Even in those days of simple but rugged technology, this was the biggest league of all, and producing and

developing a car was a specialised and expensive business. Nonetheless, Merosi set to work with a will, modifying his original chassis design, which had been used in all the production and racing A.L.F.A. models from the beginning, to incorporate new standards of lightness, toughness and compactness.

The engine, however, was a different matter. Producing a competitive car meant, most of all, designing and building a power unit capable of extracting much more power from every cubic centimetre of capacity than Merosi had been able to do with the production engines. Instead of being content with overhead valves as before, he now placed the valves as close as possible to the place where the charge of fuel-air mixture was exploded to drive the piston down the cylinder, in other words in the roof of the combustion chamber itself.

In order to make the valves as large as possible, he arranged them in two rows, each inclined at an angle to the vertical, with an almost hemispherical combustion chamber to increase the available space in the chamber roof.

For efficient combustion he placed the spark plug in the centre of the cylinder between the two rows of valves. Each row of valves was operated by a single overhead camshaft, to make the valve actuation system as simple, as efficient, and as responsive as possible.

Merosi had achieved a great deal in a short time, and with no sporting experience at this level of sophistication. The 4492cc engine delivered 88bhp, which was 17 per cent more than the 40-60 Corsa, on less than three-quarters of the capacity. But this was less than other teams were producing from similar-sized engines, and to compound the problem, the chassis and body were still too big, and much too heavy, at a total weight of 17cwt (870kg). So it was unlikely that he had produced a genuine contender for GP success – what he *had* done, though, was to set the prescription for most of the truly memorable Alfa engines for the next 60 years and more, including the power units that drove the company's most famous production, sports and GP machines over decades of unrivalled achievement.

For Merosi's 1914 Grand Prix car, however, time was fast running out. As a curtain-raiser to its sporting career, it was entered in the Circuit of Brescia. During pre-race trials it recorded a speed of 91.96mph (147.99kph), which looked fairly promising. But the promise was not to be fulfilled, for the race was never to start. Between practice and the race itself, Europe found itself at war, and motor sport events were one of the first parts of the old pre-war world to vanish for the duration.

Next to go was the market for private cars, and by 1915, when Italy joined the fighting, the company was reduced to producing 15/20HP engines to serve as stationary power generators for the Italian Army, then heavily engaged in fighting off an Austro-Hungarian attack in the northern mountains. Once again it seemed that the company's future was poor, but once again a rescuer stepped in to save the day.

This was the unlikely figure of Nicola Romeo, an industrialist and mining engineer with little interest in car-making. He was, however, a supremely shrewd and successful businessman. Within two years of his buying into the company and taking over as managing director, A.L.F.A.

Car-making soon seemed a distant, happy reminder of pre-war days

was making tractors, railway equipment, aero-engines, pumps and compressors, and Romeo had bought out the other shareholders. The company had vanished into the Romeo group, and car-making soon seemed a distant, happy reminder of pre-war days.

That was until 1918, when the tables were turned once again. The demand for most of the Romeo group's products vanished once the guns fell silent, and some use had to be found for its vast factory capacity. Cars were in short supply and the market was booming, far more quickly than the parts and raw materials could be found to satisfy it. For the time being the company was able to turn out 1914 cars from parts that had been stored at the outbreak of the war, but new designs and a new marketing policy were badly needed.

The company even needed a new name. A.L.F.A. was as outdated as the cars that carried the badge, but Romeo was linked with heavy industrial engineering and utilitarian products, with no significance for car-buying customers. The solution proved to be a brilliant compromise, combining links with the past with a

future as part of a solid engineering group respected for quality and efficiency. Alfa Romeo of Milan, one of the most famous makes in motoring history, was born.

Designing new cars to carry the name was not so simple. At first Merosi merely developed his pre-war designs, increasing their size and weight, alas beyond what was acceptable to post-war customers. He took the chassis of the 40-60, extended it, and fitted an even

Nicola Romeo, businessman rather than car enthusiast, who rescued the fledgling company and set it firmly on the road to greatness.
(Alfa Romeo archives)

heavier body to it, which took its weight up to 29.5cwt (1500kg). To power this monster, which was called the G1, he produced his first six-cylinder engine, a massive 6330cc design that threw away all of Alfa's progress by reverting to side valves, a move which, with a single carburettor, helped restrict the unit's peak power to a scarcely scintillating 70bhp.

Although this was enough to push the hefty G1 to a top speed of 70mph (113kph), the car was big and expensive, to buy and to run, and commercially it was a disaster. To the company's credit, it realised this early enough to produce a smaller and lighter version called the G2. But by then the damage was done, and this too was a failure.

Once again the company needed rescuing, this time from its own commercial mistakes. Oddly enough, salvation came as a bonus from its own motor sport efforts. In the first post-war events the competitions department had done its best with existing cars. Alfas secured class wins in the 1919 Parma to Poggio di

Berceto hillclimb, the first of a string of events to fall to the racing versions of the old 24HP and its successor, the 20-30HP, and the massive old 40-60HP war-horse. Even the 1914 Grand Prix car had its one moment of near-glory in the 275-mile (443km) *Gran Premio Gentlemen*, held as part of the 1921 Brescia Speed Week: it led the race until a massive water leak caused it to retire on the last part of the last lap.

Here too, however, the times were changing, and the cars would have to change with them. The 1921 Grand Prix formula stipulated a maximum engine size of 3 litres, which would have outlawed the old 1914 GP car in any case. So the factory set to work on a six-cylinder engine, which retreated from the overhead cams of the previous racing car in favour of pushrods and rockers for its overhead valves. With a single carburettor, the 2916cc engine delivered 56bhp, which compared well in terms of output against capacity with the more specialised 1914 design. Unfortunately, this engine too was overtaken by a change in the rules.

By the time it was ready the racing formula for the 1922 season had changed again, to a capacity limit of 2 litres.

All the same, the new engine had distinct promise as a power unit for production cars. The resulting design, the RL, the first of a remarkable series, suffered the handicap of being fitted with an even heavier body than the unsuccessful G1, but there were signs that the company was beginning to profit from its mistakes. Before long Merosi had fitted into a shorter and lighter chassis a more powerful 2994cc version of the engine, with wider bores, larger valves, stronger connecting rods and a higher compression ratio, delivering 76bhp; the result was the RLS, or RL Sport.

This was exactly the prescription that the car, and the company, needed. The top speed increased to a creditable 80mph (130kph) and demand began to increase, with production climbing to keep pace with it. The real transformation was effected by the development of a racing version, with a shorter chassis and a slim racing body. The competition engines had a higher compression ratio and later still wider cylinder bores to boost peak power to 88bhp, then 95bhp. Close-ratio gearboxes and other improvements helped raise the top speed to 90mph (145kph), and 98mph (158kph) for the racing RLTFs (for RL Targa Florio), which put the company name on the international sporting map once and for all.

The largest and most powerful of Merosi's six-cylinder pushrod RL series was the RLSS, which used an engine designed originally for a projected GP car and which itself formed the basis for a series of successful competition sports cars. This imposing 1925 version has a body by Castagna. (Alfa Romeo archives)

This they did by winning the 1923 Targa, RLTFs finishing in first, second and fourth places overall. In 1924 the engines were fitted with longer-throw cranks, increasing the capacity to 3620cc, the power to 125bhp and the top speed to 110mph (177kph). They finished second, fourth and ninth overall in the 1924 Targa, and won a list of other events. In showroom terms, production equivalents marketed as the RLS and the RLSS (RL Super Sport) sold well in their own right, and also helped boost sales of the more pedestrian RLN (for RL Normale).

Jano brought with him unrivalled flair, experience and the latest ideas in racing-car design

Nevertheless, the company's sights were still fixed firmly on the Grand Prix target. Merosi's second design, first called the GPR (for Grand Prix Romeo) but later designated the Alfa Romeo P1, returned to the inclined overhead valves, double overhead camshafts and hemispherical combustion chambers of the 1914 car. This time, however, the engine had six cylinders, with the liners fitted into a cylinder block welded up from sheet steel to save weight, and bolted to a light alloy crankcase.

A shorter and much lighter chassis and a neat, streamlined body added up to a design that was much more competitive than the earlier car had been. But with an all-up weight of 16.7cwt (850kg), the 2-litre engine's 80bhp would have a hard time outrunning opponents of the calibre of Fiat, then the team to beat in GP racing. In fact it never had the chance. Although three works cars were entered in the 1923 Italian GP, one of them, driven by Ugo Sivocci (winner of the 1923 Targa), slid off the track

during testing before the race, with fatal results. The two other cars were withdrawn as a mark of respect, and the P1 never actually ran in a race.

Perhaps it was all for the best. Merosi was a good designer of reliable production cars, but he lacked the specialised experience that was needed, even then, for a successful GP car. So a scheme was hatched to hire the engineer responsible for Fiat's GP racing cars, Vittorio Jano. Enzo Ferrari was now a works driver for Alfa, and his friend Luigi Bazzi knew Jano well. Delicate negotiations were opened and Jano moved from the Fiat workshops at Turin to the Alfa Romeo workshops in Milan.

Jano proved to be the best bargain the company recruitment department ever struck. He brought with him unrivalled flair, a fount of experience, and the latest ideas in racing-car design. His presence was to transform Alfa's racing efforts, and for the second time in the company's still short history the triumph of its racing cars was to lead to domination in the passenger-car market too, with a series of models that have come to symbolise the best of pre-war engineering and Italian design flair.

Jano's P2 Grand Prix car, seen here at a 1982 historic-car event, followed Fiat practice very closely, but won Alfa Romeo the company's first GP World Championship in 1925. (LAT)

This revolution began in the competition workshops, with an engine alarmingly similar to the straight-eight Fiat 805 racing engine that Jano had been producing in Turin. It coincided with Merosi's thinking to the extent that it had hemispherical combustion chambers, two rows of inclined valves and two overhead camshafts, but the devil was in the detail. Not only did the new engine have its 1987cc of capacity split between eight cylinders, but every precaution was taken to ensure power co-existed with reliability.

The long crankshaft was made in two pieces, was carefully counterbalanced, and was carried in ten roller bearings. Each of the camshafts was also carried in ten bearings. But the biggest change was the addition of a supercharger. Made in the company workshops and geared to run at 1.25 times engine speed, the blower was tested on the P1, where it boosted the peak power output by more than 20 per cent, to 118bhp, and pushed the car's top speed to 125mph (200kph).

The new P2 would give it a chance to do even better. The chassis was carefully refined to make the car as light and compact as possible, with minimal frontal area, and the bodywork was carefully shaped to minimise drag. The weight reduction was remarkable: even with the extra poundage of the supercharger, the P2 still weighed 2.5cwt (125kg) less than the P1, and the engine delivered a full 140bhp, producing a top speed of 140mph (224kph).

Now at last Alfa had a genuinely competitive car, and the benefits were soon to be delivered. On its first outing in June 1924 it won the Circuit of Cremona. More importantly, in August it won the Grand Prix of Europe at Lyon so convincingly that the all-conquering Fiat GP team withdrew after the event, never to enter Grand Prix racing again. It won

the Italian GP at Monza at the end of the season, achieving a brilliantly successful debut after a late start. Jano was determined that next time Alfa Romeo would win the Grand Prix World Championship.

In 1925 the P2s won the European GP at Spa in Belgium, but withdrew from the French GP following an accident that killed team driver Ascari. Nevertheless, Alfa Romeo won the Italian GP, the three works P2s finishing first, second and fourth, taking the Championship for the company. In time, and increasingly in the hands of private owners, the cars would continue to win a long list of events, culminating in Varzi's triumph in a completely revised P2 in the 1930 Targa Florio, overturning years of Bugatti domination. Yet the P2's most enduring legacy is a very different series of production models, many of which would establish a brilliant sporting record in their own right.

By the mid-1920s cars such as the RL series were too large, too thirsty and too cumbersome for many customers. First a stopgap was produced, in the form of the RM series of four-cylinder variations on the RL theme. However, what was needed was something more modern, more compact, and much easier to handle. Just as earlier racing machines had spawned the RLs, so Jano's P2 was now to sire a new line of pedigree designs. The basic decision was to take the racing engine and reduce it in size by removing two cylinders to produce a 1.5-litre 'six'.

The supercharger was also removed, and the valves arranged in a single line, driven by a single overhead camshaft. With a lower compression ratio and a single carburettor, the power output was 44bhp, so the

The first of Jano's splendid six-cylinder twin overhead cam cars, the 6C 1500. This is a 1928 roadster with split screen and upright radiator. (Alfa Romeo archives)

Jano's first production car engine for Alfa Romeo, an in-line six-cylinder with hemispherical combustion chambers and twin overhead camshafts, set a company tradition that would endure for 60 years; this is a 6C MMS unit. (LAT)

engine had a lot to do to propel a large and relatively heavy body, similar to that of the RM, at anything like a respectable speed. The first of the 6C 1500s, as the car was designated, was completed in the championship year of 1925, but production did not begin for another two years.

At first, yet again, performance was disappointing, although oddly the cars sold well from the beginning, possibly due to a close identification with the successful GP cars. But the way in which the P2 had been transformed into the 1500 meant that there was ample room for development, and there soon emerged a series of variations on the basic theme, to woo buyers with increasingly dramatic styles and more encouraging speeds and responses.

First out of the traps was the 1500 Sport, in 1928. This reverted to the hemispherical combustion chambers

and double overhead cams of the GP cars, and power climbed to 54bhp, with a top speed of 78mph (125kph). This was soon eclipsed by the shorter-wheelbase 6C 1500 Super Sport, which had a higher-compression engine delivering 60bhp and offering a top speed of 80mph (130kph). Top of the range was a supercharged version, with 76bhp and a top speed of 87mph (140kph).

Yet real performance would depend on a larger engine, and by widening the bores and lengthening the stroke Jano produced a six-cylinder unit of

1752cc, which became known to the world as the splendid Alfa 1750 series. This began exactly as the 1500 series had done, with a single-cam 46bhp version, which gave almost no sign of the good things to come. Exactly as before it was joined by a twin-cam 6C 1750 Sport, then by a Super Sport version, and finally by the 6C 1750 Gran Sport.

This delivered true performance, since its open two-seater version turned out 85bhp with the help of a supercharger, and managed a top speed of more than 90mph (145kph). In compact, closed Gran Turismo form (the first genuine GT car) it still managed 84mph (135kph), and this was far exceeded by some of the more exotic versions. By now the six-cylinder cars, like other Alfas before and since, were also having to earn their keep on the racing circuits.

The works 1750s, with fixed high-compression cylinder heads and larger valves, were turning out 102bhp, and thanks to lightened

By 1930, when this 6C 1750 four-seater tourer was made, capacity had been increased to 1752cc and the radiator raked backwards for a more sporting appearance. (LAT)

bodywork were topping 100mph (160kph) with very little effect on their natural reliability. Alfa 1750s won the 1929 and 1930 Mille Miglia races, and a host of other events.

By the end of the 1920s the company's future seemed set fair. Alongside the six-cylinder cars in all their forms (including a larger 1900cc version), it was decided that the time had come for a move upmarket. In essence what Jano did was to take the 1750 six-cylinder engine and put back the two missing cylinders to produce a 2336cc straight-eight. The clever part of the design lay in the changes he made between the original straight-eight GP car engine and the new straight-eight production unit.

Jano's beautiful straight-eight, the 8C 2300, was built in Lungo long wheelbase form and shorter Corto form, to carry close-coupled sports bodies like this immaculate roadster taking part in a classic-car re-run of the Monte Carlo Rally. (LAT)

To make the engine as simple and reliable as possible he effectively cut it in two and turned the two halves round to mount them back-to-back, with the auxiliaries in the centre. The combined unit had two four-cylinder crankshafts, and no fewer than four camshafts, each half the length of those in the P2. Each camshaft was carried in six bronze bearings, and each crankshaft in five roller bearings. The engine was fitted with a supercharger from the start, and the remarkable result of all this careful development was that the

Jano's eight-cylinder engine was really two four-cylinder units turned back-to-back with the camshaft drives under the hump in the centre of the camboxes. (LAT)

original 2300 engine delivered no less than 138bhp, which represented more power per cubic centimetre than the works racing 1750s.

Yet the beautiful 2300, which appeared in two basic forms – a *Corto* short-wheelbase version not much larger than the 1750, and the more imposing *Lungo* – was another case of a car that appeared at exactly the

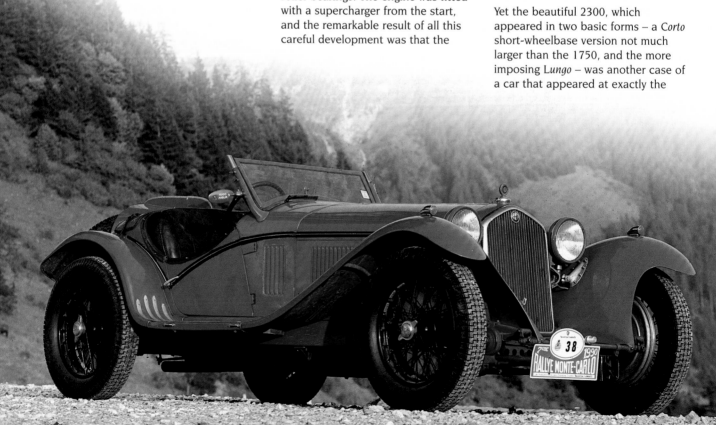

wrong time. Cars of this quality were anything but cheap, and the straight-eights cost almost twice as much as the 1750s. Moreover, the bitter winds of depression were beginning to blow from across the Atlantic, and at the very time the company was embarking on a major development programme of new models, and a return to the fiendishly expensive arena of Grand Prix racing for the first time since 1925, its loyal customers could no longer afford to buy its products.

The unpleasant truth took a long time to dawn. With the works racing 2300s given the higher compression and larger valves treatment to boost power to 155bhp, they proved to be impressive competition contenders, winning the 1931 Targa Florio and the 1932 Mille Miglia. Next on Jano's wish-list was a full-blooded racing

Jano's P3 monoposto GP car proved another world-beater, but its long-term career was blighted by the company's cash crisis in the Great Depression, and by the time the company returned to racing, victories were few against the bigger and more powerful German cars. The Alfa P3's main chassis members were curved upwards over the rear axle, and the rear wheels were driven by separate propshafts. (LAT)

version, with streamlined racing bodywork and a higher boost pressure, intended to take advantage of the new, freer Grand Prix rules.

Two of the cars were entered for the 1932 GP of Europe, held at Monza, where they finished first and second;

When the company withdrew the P3s from Grand Prix racing in 1933, the Scuderia Ferrari team had to fall back on a brilliant stopgap, a GP car in all but name that was developed from the 8C 2300 production car, and which was named the Monza after its first-time-out victory at the GP of Europe in 1931. This is a 1932 team car with the Monza's characteristic radiator slots. (LAT)

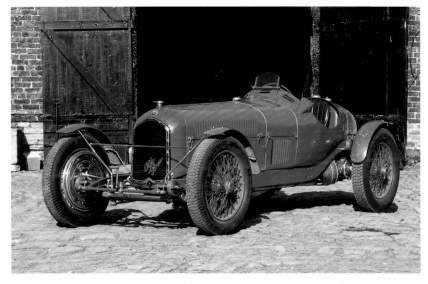

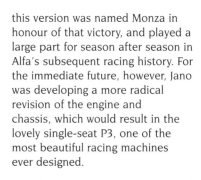

this version was named Monza in honour of that victory, and played a large part for season after season in Alfa's subsequent racing history. For the immediate future, however, Jano was developing a more radical revision of the engine and chassis, which would result in the lovely single-seat P3, one of the most beautiful racing machines ever designed.

The Monza engine was fitted with a longer-throw crankshaft, to lengthen the stroke and increase the capacity to 2654cc. With larger valves and a pair of superchargers, the power rose to 215bhp, and the dropping of the legal requirement for every racing car to carry a mechanic meant that the chassis and the elegantly streamlined body could be made much more compact. In its initial form the car was capable of 144mph (232kph), and it proved unbeatable.

During their first 1932 season the P3s failed to win overall at Marseilles and Brno, but in every other GP they triumphed, bringing Alfa Romeo its second World Championship in its first year on the circuits. At the end of the year it appeared that 1933 could only bring a repeat performance, until the economic crisis, and its effects on sales, began to bite hard. With orders tumbling, the company had to ditch all non-essential baggage to stay afloat, and

the racing programme was one of the first to go.

Yet again a rescuer was found to bail out the company. This time it was the Italian government itself, anxious not to lose such a powerful earner of overseas respect in the sporting sphere. But by the time the funds were put in place, racing had moved on. The relaxing of the capacity limits had set off a power race, which called for still more money from those who decided to take part. Increasingly the future would belong to the German Mercedes-Benz and Auto Union teams, backed by the Nazi government and boasting high-technology designs and limitless budgets.

For Alfa the rest of the 1930s would become an increasingly frustrating chase to stay abreast of the new contenders, through the introduction

of larger and more complex engines. Only occasionally would the company's efforts be crowned by the glory that Mussolini's government craved, but Alfa's army vehicles and aero-engines were increasingly important to the new rearmament programmes, so the backing of the Fascist state never faltered, right to the outbreak of war.

This had two effects on production Alfa Romeos. At first, financial prudence dictated that successors to the 1750s and 2300s had to be found, and that these should be built and sold at far more realistic prices. This process began with Jano taking the largest 1900cc engine of the six-cylinder series, increasing the bore

A roadster version of the short-chassis 8C 2900 with coachwork by Alfa Romeo itself. (LAT)

and stroke to produce a 2306cc six-cylinder unit, and fitting this into a welded box-section chassis. Carrying more practical and less exotic bodywork, the 6C 2300 could manage 75mph (120kph), a performance that, if less than overwhelming, could still be enjoyed for less than half the price of the eight-cylinder car. Orders and production climbed, to the point where the number of 6C 2300s sold in the first year of the model was more than double the four-year total of 8C 2300s.

There was even a competition version, one of which won the 24-hour race at Pescara on its first appearance; this led to the shorter, lighter GT version being named the Pescara in honour of the win. Later versions of the car had hydraulic brakes and independent front and rear suspension, and by the end of the 1930s a wider-bore version of the engine took the capacity to 2443cc, whereupon the car became known as the 6C 2500. By this time, however, the provision of cars that could hold their own in the market on commercial terms was becoming less important, so each model became more luxurious than the one before. Sport and Super Sport versions joined the range, but each model change saw production figures fall still further.

The truth was that Fascist Italy was now bent on war, and car production was beginning to be edged further into the background. It was important for national prestige that the cars that were made by Alfa Romeo were inspiring rather than commercially attractive, and specification came to matter more than sales totals. This was best summed up in one of Jano's most splendid production cars, a vehicle which took the race-bred philosophy a stage further than ever before.

This began as a sports-racing car, evolving from the all-independent chassis of the Tipo C racing car,

which had been developed as a successor to the P3. By fitting it with a 2905cc version of the 3-litre P3 engine delivering 220bhp, and creating streamlined sports bodywork, Jano and his engineers produced the Alfa 8C 2900A, a car which could reach a top speed of 143mph (230kph). Three of the first five to emerge from the works were entered in the 1936 Mille Miglia, where they finished first, second and third in another impressive demonstration of traditional Alfa reliability.

Only six of the racers were made, but a short production run of a roadgoing 2900 B model, fitted with a detuned straight-eight engine delivering 180bhp, represented some of the most exotic-looking Alfas of all time. As with the 8C 2300, there were versions with both short and long wheelbases. Twenty of the *Corto* model were made, with two-seat bodywork and a top speed of 115mph (185kph). Even rarer, and more imposing, were the 10 *Lungo* 2900 Bs, available with open, closed or cabriolet bodies and offering a top speed of 109mph (175kph) in unrivalled style.

Yet this final flowering of the company's pre-war genius appeared as Europe slid inexorably towards a

The flamboyant streamlining of the special-bodied competition version of the 8C 2900 built by Carrozzeria Touring for the 1938 Le Mans 24-Hour race. (LAT)

new war, and although the company's future seemed assured at last, it was about to face its greatest challenge of all. Until now problems had centred on lack of money, lack of customers, lack of good ideas from the design department, or lack of performance in some crucial models. This time the threat was from enemy bombers, which would leave the company's plant more than 60 per cent destroyed, and its future prospects bleak indeed.

Alfa Romeo 1900

When the war finally ended in the early summer of 1945, Alfa Romeo's Portello plant was in ruins. During the later months of the fighting, the design teams had been evacuated from Milan to escape the bombing, and had set up shop on the shores of Lake Orta to plan future models. The result of their work was an elegantly streamlined saloon called the Gazzella, which apart from its unorthodox place of birth also represented a major departure in other respects.

It was smaller, lighter and considerably less flamboyant than the last of the pre-war Alfas. It had a 2-litre engine, but delivered 85bhp, and it had a curved monocoque body with a fastback tail and room for four passengers to accompany the driver.

With all-round independent suspension, and half a ton less weight than the 2500s, top speed should have been a whisker less than 100mph, with handling to match. The Gazzella was clear proof that Alfa Romeo had at last learned from history. Here was indeed an Alfa for the future, for lower prices and bigger markets, and more in tune with the preferences of post-war buyers.

Sadly, only one prototype was ever made. When the engineers returned to the ruins of the factory, they found plenty of factory hands desperate for work, since aero engine production was barred under the peace treaty. Machine tools were wrecked, and all that remained, as with the previous war, were stacks of parts for pre-war models. So the post-war recovery

Returning self-confidence enabled Alfa to produce the *Freccia d'Oro* (Golden Arrow) closed coupé on the pre-war 6C 2500 chassis to win a broader share of the reviving post-war market. (LAT)

The original 1950 version of the Alfa Romeo 1900 saloon, the first Alfa designed for mass production, but which was assembled by hand until war-damaged machine tools could be replaced. (Alfa Romeo archives)

began with 6C 2500s being assembled by hand, detuned to cope with the limited supplies of poor quality petrol then available.

Yet the promise of the Gazzella was not forgotten. When the time came to replace the 2500s, as it would when the stocks of parts ran out and when new machine tools made more radical designs possible, the new car would have to represent a sharp break with many of the traditions of the past. It would have a true monocoque body, and be a genuine four-seater saloon with neat though understated styling for good aerodynamics. To keep weight and price down, the interior would be austere compared with past Alfas, and it would be fitted with a rigid rear axle, also on the grounds of cost and simplicity.

Nevertheless, some qualities of the new car were too essential to allow any compromise. The engine was a four-cylinder unit, but it still had the classic Alfa Romeo recipe of twin overhead camshafts and

Alfa Romeo 1900
1950-1953

ENGINE:
Four-cylinder, twin ohc
Bore x stroke	82.55 x 88mm
Capacity	1884cc
Power	90bhp

TRANSMISSION:
Four-speed gearbox
Final drive	4.1:1

BODY STYLE:
Four-door saloon

PERFORMANCE:
(from contemporary sources)
Max speed	106mph (170kph)
0–60mph (97kph)	18.6 seconds

LENGTH:	14ft 6in (4.42m)
WIDTH:	5ft 3in (1.60m)
WHEELBASE:	8ft 8in (2.64m)

1900 Super
1953-59

As 1900 except:
Bore x stroke	84.5 x 88mm
Capacity	1975cc
Max speed	100mph (160kph)

1900 TI
1951-53

As 1900 except:
Power	100bhp
Max speed	106mph (170kph)
0–60mph (97kph)	17.5 seconds

1900 TI Super
1953-57

As 1900 Super except:
Power	115bhp
Max speed	112mph (180kph)
0–60mph (97kph)	17.0 seconds

NUMBER BUILT:
1900	7,611
1900 Super	8,282
1900 TI	572
1900 TI Super	478
1900 Sprint/Super Sprint	1,894
1900 Primavera coupé	300

The classic Alfa Romeo twin overhead camshaft in-line engine in its new post-war four-cylinder form. (Peter Marshall)

particular to very high temperatures, as they swirled out of the cylinders on the exhaust stroke. To ensure that the engines could stand up to sustained high-speed running on autostrada journeys therefore meant borrowing from Alfa's aero-engine experience, and using valve stems of chrome plate over a sodium core, together with valve seats made from stellite alloy.

The ingenuity of the 1900 engine was in its combination of racing-car layout – for greater efficiency – with materials and details that allowed mass-production prices and

The basic engine design would serve the company well over the next four decades

promised mass-production reliability. Yet its output per cubic centimetre was almost as high as the specialised, highly-tuned and supercharged Gran Sport 1750s of 20 years before, and this at the very start of the 1900's development. Furthermore, the basic engine design would serve the company well over the next four decades in a whole range of classic models.

hemispherical combustion chambers. With a capacity of 1884cc it delivered 90bhp, enough to provide a car weighing 21.7cwt (1100kg) with a top speed of 93mph (150kph). This combination of traditional virtues and forward thinking was to revitalise the company's fortunes – under the name Alfa Romeo 1900.

The first 1900s appeared in 1950, although continuing shortages of machine tools meant that the first production cars were still largely hand-assembled. Parts were scarce too, and the original engine capacity was based on bores of 3.25 inches, or 82.55mm, for the British-sourced Hepolite pistons that had to be used in place of locally made components. The engine had a cast-iron cylinder block with wet cylinder liners, and a crankcase formed as part of the block casting.

Because the 1900 engine was designed to deliver more power by burning more fuel and running faster than its pre-war predecessors, greater quantities of hot gases tended to heat the exhaust valves in

The body was a simple three-box, four-door design with bench seats front and rear. To provide more interior room, the gearchange was on the steering column, and there was no sign of the wooden dashboard and soft carpets of the final pre-war models. The 1900 was finished in painted metal and fitted with rubber mats, with only a tall and narrow stylised version of the Alfa radiator shield to establish who had made the car.

The last of the pre-war Alfas had had independent suspension front and rear, with dampers that could be adjusted from inside the car to deliver the right combination of ride comfort and handling precision. The 1900 turned its back on all that. While the front suspension retained the coil springs of the 2500, in conjunction with single top links and lower wishbones, and hydraulic dampers, the rear wheels were carried on a solid axle, which might seem a determined step backwards.

In fact, the Alfa rear suspension was a carefully thought-out compromise that, once again, was to last well into the 1970s. Cost was of paramount importance, and since the cheapest independent rear suspension was the swing-axle system, which could produce sharp camber changes under cornering loads, with disastrous effects on a car's handling, the engineers opted instead for a solid axle to ensure that track and camber remained constant, but located it with great care to provide precise handling.

Suspended on coil springs, movement of the axle was restricted by fitting two rods that ran from a mounting point on the top of the differential to

The dashboard of the Fangio 1900 Sprint. (Peter Marshall)

box sections at the side of the floor-pan. Not only did this reduce axle tramp and hop, but it also transferred part of the weight of the differential (which contributed most of the weight of the rear suspension) from the suspension to the chassis. This reduced unsprung weight at the expense of sprung weight, in the interests of better roadholding.

By 1951 Alfa Romeo's plans for mass production were being paralleled by the revival of the independent coachbuilders, who were producing a variety of bodies on the 1900 chassis. This is a 1900 Sprint coupé by Touring, built in 1951 for Argentine racing driver Juan Manuel Fangio. (Peter Marshall)

Initially the 1900s emerged from the Portello workshops at a glacial three cars per day. Later, as more machine tools were installed and improvements made, the rate increased, but only a handful had been completed by the end of 1950; despite this, detail improvements were already being made. The prototypes had been shown to the press at the Turin exhibition centre in May of that year, but the model's first proper motor show appearance was at the Paris Show of the following October, then at the London Motor Show later that same month, thanks to Frazer Nash who donated stand space. Already, *The Autocar* noted with approval that 'subtle changes in wing lines, radiator grille and bumpers have greatly improved the appearance of the Alfa Romeo 1900 saloon since the prototype was seen in the spring'.

During the following year more and more 1900s emerged from the works, with the 1951 annual total amounting to 1,220 saloons, an all-time record for the company. Demand was such that no cars were available for the British market, although *The Autocar* was able to try a car in Italy, and thoroughly enjoyed the experience. The magazine reported that the steering was 'superb', that the engine was smooth and flexible and that the car handled well with moderate understeer and 'very little body roll'. It was disappointed by the interior trim and finish, which it described as 'simple, almost austere', but was confident that 'enthusiasts for the make will find that the 1900 remains an Alfa in spirit'.

In those days motor magazines were so subtle in their criticism that one has to read between the lines to

The catalogued cabriolet on the 1900C floorpan was by Pininfarina, and most wore wire wheels. Separate company Stabilimenti Farina built some cabrios on the standard 1900 chassis, with its longer wheelbase.
(Alfa Romeo archives)

judge opinions accurately. The testers reported that 'it lacks the appearance of luxury associated with the more glamorous pre-war models, and the simplicity and finish of its equipment may cause casual observers to question its price. It is not the quietest car in its class . . . but for those who drive fast and far, and look beyond the superficial to the engineering essentials, it would be difficult to find such a combination of speed, stability and fuel economy anywhere else at the price.'

The 1900 lacks the appearance of luxury associated with the glamorous pre-war models

The figures spoke volumes, by the standards of the time. The basic production saloon reached 60mph from a standing start in 17.1 seconds. It reached a top speed of 105mph (169kph) on test (which suggests that something was distinctly non-standard about the test car) and recorded a fuel consumption of 17mpg when driven hard. These were outstanding measures of the car's performance, and sales had already begun to increase, to the point where the company could start considering additions to the range.

In 1951 the *Turismo Internazionale*, or TI, version appeared, named after a popular class of Italian saloon car racing. The alterations were limited to larger valves, a fractionally higher compression ratio, and a double-choke carburettor instead of the original single-choke unit. Even without any change in the number of carburettors or the capacity of the engine, this was enough to boost peak power to 100bhp, and the official top speed increased to 106mph (171kph), with brisker acceleration to match.

Dr Orazio Satta Puliga

During the pre-war period Alfa Romeo had employed a succession of engineers to design its cars, starting with Merosi and Jano. When Jano left in September 1937, after the failure of the racing car programme to catch up with the all-conquering German teams, he was replaced by Gioacchino Colombo in the racing department, and a former aero-engine designer called Bruno Trevisan in the passenger car department, together with a Spanish engineer, Wilfredo Ricart, later to design the Spanish '50s supercar, the Pegaso, in charge of special projects. Born in 1897, Ricart had worked in Spain, designing and building cars and engines, and running the public transport system in Valencia until 1936, when Alfa Romeo employed him as a technical adviser, to design a diesel engine, a pair of aero-engines and a range of sports and racing prototypes, culminating in the Gazzella.

For the vital 1900 project, however, the company turned to a young engineer called Dr Orazio Satta Puliga, known to his colleagues simply as Satta. After studying mechanical and aeronautical engineering at Turin Polytechnic, Satta had been appointed Assistant Professor in the aeronautical engineering department of the

Dr Orazio Satta Puliga, designer of the classic post-war Alfa Romeos from the 1900 to the Alfetta. (Alfa Romeo archives)

college, before joining Alfa Romeo in 1938 at the age of 27.

In 1946 he was promoted to Manager of the Experimental and Design departments, and his was the inspiration behind the 1900 and its variants. In his 34-year career with the company, he was responsible for a whole succession of classic Alfa Romeos, including the Giulietta and Giulia models, the revised Alfetta GP cars, the 33 sports-racing cars, the 1750 and 2000 series, and the Alfetta road cars.

Another Touring coupé with very
similar details to the Fangio car, this
time based on a 1954 1900C Super
Sprint chassis. (Peter Marshall)

Not much post-war austerity in this
shot of the dashboard and interior of a
coachbuilt 1900C Super Sprint. (Peter
Marshall)

An example of the bespoke coachwork available on the 1900C – or *Corto* – floorpan, this is a 1953 coupé bodied by Ghia. (LAT)

With sales and production continuing to increase, Alfa also took a tentative step back in the direction of its pre-war philosophy. By making a slightly shorter version of the 1900 floorpan, with a wheelbase of 8ft 2in (2.5m) instead of the 8ft 7in (2.63m) of the production model, and making it available to the ranks of Italy's superb coachbuilders, the company was able to provide for those with the taste, and the means, for something more exotic and more comfortable.

This version of the car was called the Sprint, and provided the basis for a wide range of designs from Italy's specialist coachbuilders. On a series basis, Pininfarina turned out an elegant cabriolet, and Touring produced a two-door, two-seat closed coupé, both of which provided a touch of exclusivity at a price 25 per cent above that of the standard car. In all, 949 Sprints were made, together with another 91 cars identified in Alfa's records as 1900 Cabriolets. Although the cabriolet's extra stiffening, to cope with the open top, added another 2cwt (100kg), top speed remained the same. The coupé was the same weight as the TI but, thanks to better aerodynamics, was actually faster, with a top speed of 112mph (180kph).

By 1954 just over 10,000 1900s had been made. The car was available in Britain, and a series of detailed changes toned down the uncompromising austerity of the original versions. Additionally, the engine capacity was increased, by enlarging the bores to 84.5mm, which produced an engine of 1975cc; this was just as well, as the weight of the car had increased appreciably.

The 1900M

The intention with the 1900 series was to enable mass-production economies to bring the price down to a level that made sense in the post-war market. Nonetheless, there was scope for Alfa Romeo to develop special versions for different customers. There were specially equipped 1900 police cars, and a four-door convertible prototype aimed at the Army for staff-car use. The most versatile and the most utilitarian was the 1900M or Matta, Alfa Romeo's nearest equivalent to the Land Rover.

During the early part of the war, when Mussolini still had plans for a new Roman Empire in Africa, Alfa had produced a rugged open-top Jeep-like version of the 6C 2500 called the Coloniale. With all-round independent suspension and a limited-slip differential driving the rear wheels, two prototypes did well on tests, and the Italian War Ministry ordered 150. By the time the last had been delivered, the Italian presence in Africa had come to an end, and no more were made.

In 1951 the Italian Army was in the market again, looking for an all-purpose reconnaissance vehicle that could be used on and off normal roads. The result was a much more Jeep-like vehicle based on a welded floortray, stiffened by longitudinal and transverse box sections, and using the 1900 twin-cam engine. It was detuned to 65bhp, and was fitted with a wider-ratio four-speed gearbox, normally driving the rear wheels. When the going became especially rough, 4WD could be selected via a two-speed transfer box.

The chassis was shorter and narrower than that of the 1900, and the coil-spring rear suspension was replaced by a transverse semi-elliptic leaf spring. Top speed was a useful 65mph (105kph) and 2000 were ordered and supplied to the Army as the Alfa Romeo AR51 during 1952 and 1953. Another 12 of these vehicles were turned out by the company, followed by 154 of the AR52 civilian version during 1954. Some were fitted to haul farm machinery, others were fitted with

snow-ploughs or used as fire tenders. Finally, one was given an estate-car body, complete with hard top and strakes along the body panels, with the idea of producing a very short-coupled compact delivery vehicle for shops and market gardeners.

Built for the Italian army, the AR51 or Matta used a detuned 1900 engine – quite an aristocratic unit for an off-roader! – and featured selectable four-wheel drive; rear springing was by transverse leaf rather than the 1900's coils. (Peter Marshall)

The 1900 Super Primavera pillarless coupé was an adaptation by Boano available as a catalogued Alfa model, and was offered, as the regular Super, with two-tone bodywork. (Peter Marshall)

boosted the peak power to 115bhp at 5500rpm, and the top speed increased to 112mph (180kph); nonetheless this version was also offered at a 16 per cent reduction in price over the previous TI.

Together with the increased performance and reduced prices, the cars were embellished with fashionable styling details such as extra chrome around the windows and waistline, and even two-tone bodywork. The 1900 Sprint had now become the 1900 Super Sprint, and was attracting the attention of a wider circle of coachbuilders. Variations were built by Boano, Boneschi, Ghia and Zagato, in addition to established collaborators Touring and Pininfarina.

To anyone used to the later front-gearbox Alfas, the 1900 will seem a very different animal. Lacking the delicacy in its responses of a Giulietta or Giulia, the 1900 feels almost vintage. In place of the delicious revviness of, say, the Giulietta's little 1290cc power unit, the 1900's 'big four' has lots of gutsy low-down torque and a turbine-like delivery. A

The saloon was now known as the 1900 Super. Despite an unchanged peak power output, the top speed climbed from 93mph (150kph) to 99mph (159kph), while the benefits of mass-production economics were passed on to customers through cutting the price by 16 per cent.

Meanwhile the TI was given a more comprehensive update, to produce the TI Super. The engine compression ratio was raised to 8:1 and a pair of double-choke carburettors fitted, while separate exhaust tracts for each cylinder improved gas flow. All this

This 1900 Super Sprint carries Touring's second style of closed coachwork and was produced from 1956 to 1958. (Alfa Romeo archives)

Flying saucers and BATmobiles

In spite of its unassuming exterior, the 1900 served as the basis for some of the most exotic vehicles ever built on Alfa Romeo chassis. The first of these was a works project, for a sports-racing car using the 1900 engine and mechanical parts. This was the Alfa Romeo C52 *Disco Volante*, or Flying Saucer. A 1900 engine had the bores enlarged to 85mm, increasing the capacity to 1997.4cc, ideal for the 2-litre racing class. With twin double-choke carburettors, a higher compression ratio and sharper cam profiles, the engine delivered 158bhp at 6500rpm.

But the most unusual feature of the *Disco Volante* was its body. This was built on a tubular space frame fitted with uprated 1900 front and rear suspension units. A specially shaped undertray was wind-tunnel tested to reduce to a minimum turbulence and drag below the car, and three different body styles were tried out. An open two-seater and a closed

The closed coupé version of the *Disco Volante*. (Alfa Romeo archives)

coupé both had an extremely unusual egg-like cross-section, supposedly to reduce the influence of sidewinds but more probably a styling quirk. The third was a more conventionally shaped coupé intended for hillclimb events.

The car was first shown at the New York International Motor Sport Show

in the spring of 1953. However, it never fulfilled its promise of a genuine top speed of 135mph (216kph), since the aerodynamics proved rather too efficient – at generating rear-end lift – with dramatic effects on its handling. As a

Bertone produced a series of designs, with a bizarre mix of fins and channels

competition car the *Disco Volante* was a failure, but the variations remain among the most unusual and futuristic designs ever produced by the company.

The second strange variation on the 1900 theme was an outside project, by Carrozzeria Bertone. It was a design exercise called the Berlina Aerodinamica Tecnica, or BAT, which

The open roadster version of the 1900-based *Disco Volante*. (LAT)

was intended to reverse the *Disco Volante* airflow problem by channelling air over the car's body so that it actually increased the pressure of the wheels on the road at speed, thus improving the roadholding.

A series of different designs, with bizarre combinations of fins and channels, were completed up to the summer of 1953. Accounts differ as to whether these comprised five or seven different designs, Bertone's policy being to base each design on

the same 1900 Super Sprint chassis to give an objective starting point for comparison of how each handled. Although problems of visibility and public taste prevented the designs from having much effect on the styling of production cars, the knowledge gained from tailfins in particular proved useful for racing prototypes in later years.

The bizarre BAT series of aerodynamic prototypes built by Bertone around 1900 mechanical parts. (LAT)

The 1900 in competition

In 1951 Alfa retired from GP racing after winning the company's fourth World Championship. However, to keep the company name alive among motor sport enthusiasts it was decided to mount a scaled-down competition effort based on the 1900. In that same year a production 1900 saloon was driven on what was called a 'Raid' (really a long-distance endurance trip) from Milan to the toe of Italy, by ship to Tripoli in North Africa, then across the desert and the mountains of Ethiopia to Somalia and the port of Mogadishu. The car stood up to the harsh climate and the rough roads encouragingly well.

The next step was to enter a TI in the 1952 Mille Miglia, where Sanesi finished third in his class in a 1900 Sprint with a Touring coupé body. (In that same event, the 1900M off-roader actually won its class, which was restricted to military vehicles, so the competition was probably a great deal less formidable.) Although the 1900s were soon overtaken by larger and more ambitious specialist prototypes, they continued to do well in the hands of private drivers in rallies and touring car events all over Europe. For example, in 1954 Corini and Sanesi drove a pair of 1900 TIs in the Carrera Mexicana, and Corini and Artesoni paired up in a single 1900 TI for class wins in the Mille Miglia and the Tour of Sicily.

The 1900 TI that won first place in the Touring class in the 1954 Tour de France. (Alfa Romeo archives)

relatively heavy car, its handling lacks the poise of later cars, but the steering is still agreeably precise, the brakes are good, and the column change one of the best you are likely to encounter. Interior detailing – even on the humble saloons – is typical of

In terms of previous production totals, the 1900 took Alfa into a new league

Italian cars of the era, melding austerity with some splendidly artistic detailing in a way no British mid-ranger of the period ever achieved.

The 1900 range remained in production until 1959, by which time a total of 21,304 cars of all versions had been made. Alfa's own plans had originally been based on an annual production run of more than 12,000 cars, so the output had fallen far short of that target, and 1900s remained vary rare indeed outside Italy. But in terms of previous production totals, the 1900 took Alfa Romeo into a new league, and served the company well. As early as the end of 1954 more 1900s had been built than all other production Alfa Romeos put together, and the models that were to succeed it would extend that output still further, and become much more familiar classics on the roads of the world.

Buying Hints

1. Only a handful of 1900s survive in the UK. If you want one, try looking in Italy with the help of a magazine such as *Auto d'Epoca* or *Ruoteclassiche*. Your first port-of-call, however, should be the British-based Alfa Romeo 1900 Register.

2. Parts for the 1900 engine are less easy to locate than for later engines, and are not cheap, but the iron-block unit lasts well; as with all Alfa engines, rattly timing chains are common. The Solex twin-choke carburettors on Super Sprints can be temperamental and parts for them are not always easy to find.

3. The gearbox is essentially the same as on all front-gearbox Alfas other than the very early Giuliettas and their Sprint/Spider derivatives; it is prone to the traditional Alfa malady of weak synchromesh on second. The column change (a five-speed floor shift is found on some Super Sprints) suffers from worn bushes and stretch in the operating cable; restoring the shift's precision is down to expert fettling by a specialist.

4. The brake master cylinder is shared with other Alfas and thus easy to find. Wheel cylinders are less easy, but Alfa specialists can generally locate them.

5. Be cautious if there is wear in the kingpins – the 1900 and derived 2000/2600 use kingpin swivels rather than the balljoints of later cars. Supplies of replacement kingpins have almost dried up, which means that you have to pay a high price either for a genuine set or to have pins and bushes made from scratch.

6. All suspension bushing is obtainable, with some bush sizes being shared with the Giulietta and Giulia.

7. The saloon's steel monocoque body is immensely sturdy. Water can sit in the floors and rot them out, and, as with any car, the door bottoms and wheelarches are vulnerable to corrosion.

8. The aluminium panelling of Sprint coupés brings with it the possibility of sacrificial corrosion where steel underframing meets alloy skin. The door apertures, sills and wheelarches are key areas for inspection.

Alfa Romeo
Giulietta

In spite of the undoubted virtues of the 1900, it was the model that succeeded it that represented a major step forward for Alfa Romeo in two respects. The Giulietta, introduced late in 1954, was a return to Alfas that looked elegant rather than utilitarian. It was also the first truly mass-produced Alfa. Despite all the plans for the 1900, this had never reached its production targets, and more Giuliettas would be sold in its third full year of production than all the 1900s ever made. The new car was named after Juliet, the partner of Romeo in Shakespeare's play, and in a determined statement of the company's intentions for the future, the first version to appear was not the saloon, but the sleekly-styled Giulietta Sprint coupé (see Chapter 4).

The delayed Giulietta saloon finally made its debut in April 1955, and was a revelation. Although it had a strong family resemblance to its 1900 predecessor, it looked markedly sleeker, faster and infinitely more modern, and proved to be a shape that dated very little. With a slightly

The Giulietta seemed much higher off the ground than its 1900 predecessor; note the original style of small tail lamps. (Alfa Romeo archives)

The Giulietta saloon managed to maintain a distinct family resemblance to the 1900, but with lighter and more modern lines in keeping with mid-1950s fashion. (Alfa Romeo archives)

Giulietta Berlina
1955–1963

ENGINE:
Four-cylinder, twin ohc
Bore x stroke	74 x 75mm
Capacity	1290cc
Power	53bhp

TRANSMISSION:
Four-speed gearbox
Final drive 4.56:1

PERFORMANCE:
Max speed	88mph (140kph)
0–60mph	19.6 seconds

LENGTH:	13ft 2in (4.01m)
WIDTH:	5ft 2in (1.57m)
HEIGHT:	4ft 8in (1.42m)

Giulietta TI
1957–1964

As Giulietta Berlina except:
Power	65–74bhp
Max speed (65bhp model)	97mph (155kph)
0–60mph (97kph)	17.7 seconds

NUMBER BUILT:
Giulietta Berlina	39,057
Giulietta TI	92,728

narrower track and a shorter wheelbase, it weighed a lean 18cwt (915kg), which was a good 4cwt (200kg) less than the 1900. This was just as well, as it was powered by a much smaller version of the 1900's twin-overhead-cam four, delivering considerably less power.

Surprisingly, performance suffered relatively little. The Giulietta engine used the same basic configuration as the 2-litre, but the block was cast in light alloy, with removable steel cylinder liners. Bore and stroke were set almost square at 74mm by 75mm giving a total capacity of just 1290cc. With a 7.5 to 1 compression ratio, and a single downdraught carburettor, the engine delivered 53bhp at 5500rpm, which was a lower bhp-per-litre figure than that of the 1900. Nevertheless, it was enough to give the car a top speed of 87mph (140kph), which was fast enough to appeal to sporting-minded drivers, especially when combined with Alfa handling.

The Giulietta inherited the 1900's combination of an independent front end with a carefully located solid rear axle, and like the 1900 it rolled mightily on the entrance to a sharp bend, then gripped the road well, its ultimate cornering power being remarkably high. To tame the initial roll a front anti-roll bar was fitted.

Inside, the finish was still somewhat austere, with rubber mats, bench seats and a steering-column

Test reports on the Berlina were full of praise for its fine road behaviour

gearchange, which led some overseas testers to claim that the saloon was made solely with the home market in mind. Certainly they complained about the car's price, although they agreed that the small but efficient engine made for low taxation (in countries where this was dependent on engine capacity) and low fuel costs. They also praised the front seat legroom and the luggage space.

Everyone agreed that the best thing about the Giulietta Berlina was its road behaviour. Phrases like 'precise steering' and 'superb brakes', and roadholding described as 'hardly to be compared with any other machine in its class' were sprinkled liberally through test reports. There was

The interior design and appointments were still austere. (Peter Marshall collection)

almost universal agreement that this was a car at the start of its development process, with an engine that was extremely under-exploited, and calls were made for a more performance-minded version.

In the summer of 1955 the beautiful and almost ageless Giulietta Spider appeared (see Chapter 4), and having to share the market with two such desirable sporting variants made the saloon appear very much the poor relation of the model range. What was clearly needed was a Giulietta equivalent of the 1900 TI, and in 1957 this duly appeared as the Giulietta TI. The prescription was simple: take a Giulietta Berlina body and running gear, and replace the basic engine with the higher-compression and more ambitiously carburetted version used in the Spider.

This engine had the same bore and stroke as the Berlina, but with an 8 to 1 compression ratio and a double-choke carburettor now delivered a slightly more lively 63bhp at 6000rpm.

RIGHT:
The late model Giulietta TI as produced from 1961 to 1964; the slightly finned rear wing treatment had been introduced in 1957, on the first TI. (LAT)

This was enough to cut the time to 60mph from a standing start by 3 seconds to 11.5 seconds, and to raise the top speed to a genuine 96mph (154kph), although some road-testers found the car actually exceeded this in practice.

The interior was still spartan, with rubber mats and fabric-upholstery bench seats, and a steering-column change for the four-speed gearbox. The speedometer was a shallow-arc curve across the top of the steering column rather than a round dial, but

Advertising also stressed the amount of space inside the car, with bench seats front and rear and a steering-column-mounted gearchange. (Peter Marshall collection)

the TI version also carried a tachometer and an oil pressure gauge, as well as temperature gauges for both oil and water. More unusual features included a hand throttle, and a headlight-flasher button in the centre of the steering wheel.

With the performance boost the car's responses received universal praise. The lightness and accuracy of the steering, the balance and tenacity of the roadholding and the free acceleration delivered by the smooth, flexible and responsive engine all added up to a highly marketable proposition. As with any design, there were some weaknesses: a high noise level at speed and a stiff ride at the rear were two prices paid for this injection of additional performance into a lightweight body/chassis. Furthermore, drivers found that play in the complex linkages of the column gearchange made shifts up and down the box slower and more difficult than with a floor-mounted gearlever.

Ultimately the Giulietta TI proved to be the most popular model in the range. Of a total production of

177,690 Giuliettas, the standard Berlina accounted for 39,057 (or 22 per cent), but this was dwarfed by the TI, of which 92,728 were made – more than 50 per cent of the total, meaning it outsold all other Giulietta models put together. Some idea of the relative importance of the UK market is shown by the minuscule total of 780 Giulietta TIs turned out in right-hand-drive form – fewer than one per cent of the total output!

In 1959 the whole range was given a series of detailed engine improvements. Accompanied by the adoption of a more robust 1900-derived gearbox, these changes made no difference to the claimed power output, being intended to make the engines stronger and more reliable. The company considered the modifications important enough to change the whole Giulietta numbering scheme: where the previous cars had model numbers in the 750 series (apart from the TI with a 753 model number) those fitted with the new engines carried numbers beginning with 101 instead.

This 1959 Giulietta estate was one of a series built by Carrozzeria Colli. (Alfa Romeo archives)

Also in 1959 the TI received detail changes. The fuel pump was moved from the upper front section of the bonnet to below the distributor, and the petrol filler cap was moved to the right rear wing. The body was given recessed headlamps, moulding strips to stiffen the bonnet lid, side air intakes embellished with polished chrome strips, and rubber guards on the bumpers; there were also new direction indicators and rear lights, a new number plate lamp, and a 'Giulietta TI' logo on the boot. Inside, the car had a revised dashboard, with a strip-type speedometer and a tachometer, together with oil and water temperature gauges, and there were padded sunvisors and an interior light controlled by the front doors.

The Giulietta looked like an Italian saloon but felt like an exotic sporting machine

In 1961 the TI was given a more powerful engine. The compression ratio was raised to 8.5 to 1, and with a revised exhaust system the power increased to 74bhp at 6200rpm. This sharpened the acceleration rather than increasing the top speed. At the same time the Giulietta body received a new front treatment with mesh-like auxiliary grilles incorporating the direction indicator lights, and a larger boot. The separate front seats now had fully reclining backs, with wide net pockets on the seatbacks and ashtrays on the rear door panels. More important from the driver's viewpoint was the gearchange, which was now controlled on the TI by a long but relatively precise floor lever.

Because of the Giulietta's short wheelbase and compact dimensions, the passengers sat very upright, which accounted for the car's high stance on the road. Together with the

Why the Sprint came out first...

The reasons for this reversal of the normal practice were linked to Alfa's continuing post-war cash crisis. So short were company funds that the only way to fund the development of the new car was to organise a lottery, where entrants would hand over their money in large quantities for the chance to win one of the new models. This worked very well until the inevitable development delays pushed the launch date further and further back. Alfa Romeo was caught with zabaglione on its face by revealing the winners' names before there were enough cars completed to hand over as prizes.

This left the company facing a public relations disaster of enormous proportions. Fortunately, the chassis, mechanicals and engines were ready, so as a stopgap the coachbuilder Nuccio Bertone was commissioned to produce a sleek and streamlined 2+2 coupé body design. This was fitted to enough sets of parts to provide the promised prizes, and the car was announced to the waiting world as the Alfa Romeo Giulietta Sprint in late 1954. Real success, and series production of a design that started literally as a cover-up exercise, still lay ahead.

car's high rear roll centre, which was reinforced by fixing the triangular member locating the solid rear axle to the top of the differential housing, this conspired to produce a sideways movement on bumpy roads. As with the earlier Giuliettas, the TI version relied on large finned drum brakes rather than discs, but they were invariably slow to show any signs of fade, even under the harshest of conditions.

Most contemporary road tests agreed on the sporting appeal of the car. In August 1961 T*he Motor* summed up the feelings of many when it wrote of the right-hand-drive version, which then sold for a substantial £1645 on the UK market: 'Unique and very Italian in its character, this model is astonishingly fast, reasonably quiet, and has a moderate thirst for fuel; it is rather uncomfortable for passengers but exceptionally controllable and gives every impression of being built for hard work.' The testers also spoke of 'oddly arranged controls with unconventional responses which give some people a very poor first impression, but once familiar with the

Giulietta, drivers are often reluctant to go back to more normal types of motoring.'

What the Giulietta prescription really added up to was the body style of an Italian saloon with enough elegance in its lines to set it apart from most of its contemporaries (the late 1950s was arguably not one of the best periods for automobile styling), and with the feel and responses of a much more exotic piece of sporting machinery, all – in its home country – at a relatively competitive price. The fact that its sporting ancestry was shown in subtle but effective ways, such as in the design and layout of the uncompromisingly thoroughbred engine and in the carefully set up suspension system, merely added to its appeal for the new breed of enthusiasts. This was to become one of the enduring Alfa themes of the post-war years, and a powerful combination that would keep customers queuing for each new model for decades to come. Unmistakably, this trend was begun by the saloon and TI versions of the Giulietta.

In spite of its performance appeal, the interior of the Giulietta TI was as understated as the outside, and the strip speedometer persisted even after the bench seat and the steering-column gearchange had been replaced by separate seats and a floor-mounted lever. (LAT)

By the early 1960s the design had matured to the point where noise and vibration had been tamed relative to the levels of the earlier cars. The switch from a column to a floor gearchange gave drivers the chance to experience the pleasures of precise control over a gearbox that, notwithstanding the choice of the then normal four speeds, enabled them to use the willingness of the engine to the full. All four speeds had synchromesh, and limiting the change points to an engine speed of 5000rpm produced maximum speeds in the intermediate gears of 23mph, 40mph and 57mph.

As would become progressively familiar to drivers of later Alfa models, the gearlever was spring-biased towards the third–fourth gear plane, as an extra safeguard against incorrect shifts. Furthermore, the positions and range of movement of

the pedals made heel-and-toe operation during downshifts easier.

'It is possible to dislike quite strongly the rather jerky way in which it gets from place to place, regarding its talent for reaching any required destination in an exceptionally short time as no more than a slight extenuating circumstance,' commented The Motor. The magazine softened this fairly sharp criticism, by the standards of the time, by going on to say 'It is equally possible to find that the speed and controllability of this vivacious saloon have put the fun back into motoring.'

While testing an identical-specification car a matter of weeks earlier, The Autocar found the front seats uncomfortable because of short cushions and padding in the wrong place. The rear seats were much better, but legroom was restricted,

Giuliettas in competition

From the introduction of the Giulietta TI, competition versions of the car were to take over from the ranks of the private owners of Giulietta Sprints in production-car events all over Europe. In the especially tough Alpine Rally of 1958, for example, 58 cars started, but only 25 managed to finish. Overall winner was a French-entered Sprint, but the cars that finished second and third were Giulietta TIs entered by French and German teams.

The car proved especially good for rallying, where its relatively high ground clearance was a distinct bonus. Later in 1958 Mesdames Aumas and Wagner won the Ladies' Prize in the Tour of Corsica. In the following year a TI, entered in the standard and modified touring-car class, won the Lyons–Charbonnières Rally, and the year after that Greder and de Lageneste won the Geneva Rally in yet another TI.

A Giulietta TI trying very hard indeed in the 1959 Lyons–Charbonnières Rally. (Alfa Romeo archives)

especially when the front seat was pushed back. Otherwise the magazine's findings agreed with those of most other testers in praising the low level of wind noise and the virtual immunity from brake fade. On the other hand, it claimed that body roll was only noticeable if a corner was entered late and fast. With a smooth transition from the straight, the car tended to remain much more level.

So far as the sideways hops on hitting bumps were concerned, these seemed to be an inherent consequence of the compromises made in opting for a solid rear axle, however carefully located. The Autocar emphasised that 'on such surfaces minor deviation occurred whenever one rear wheel was deflected, which resulted in a slight corkscrew motion'. In contrast, when fully laden, and with the tyres pumped up to the recommended higher pressures, observed the magazine, 'the ride becomes much smoother, the rear passengers being more comfortable than those at the front. On roads with really deep potholes, the car could be driven at quite high speeds without any significant loss of steering control, and in these severe conditions the body structure proved to be very rigid'.

A marked degree of body roll was no bar to tenacious handling on all Alfas, particularly so with the Giulietta TI; the mesh-like side grilles identify this car as a '61–'64 third-series model. (LAT)

The *Autocar*'s final remarks could almost have been written by Alfa Romeo's Marketing Department, so closely did they agree with the company's philosophy for the design. 'British manufacturers do not produce a model comparable with the Giulietta, and few of its competitors in world markets can match it for performance, safety in handling, and running economy'.

The standard Giulietta was discontinued in 1963, the TI the following year. In nine years of full production these modest-looking saloons had attracted enough customers to provide a solid commercial basis for the more exotic and eagerly sought-after Sprints and

Spiders, and had laid a secure foundation for their even more successful replacement, the bigger and more powerful Giulia range.

The Giulietta set the template for all future front-gearbox Alfas, to the point where the glib judgement 'they all drive the same, these Alfas', cannot readily be dismissed. But that is no real criticism, because the self-effacing looks of the Giulietta hide a seductive nature.

Some might be inclined to write off the 1290cc twin-cam as not quite up to the job of propelling 18.5cwt of four-door saloon, but in fact it is a willing, free-revving delight, capable in late TI form of pushing the Giulietta to close-on 100mph and offering impressive mid-range muscle. The column change is no hardship, while the floor change, with its beefy non-remote lever, has impeccable directness and a satisfying lightness as it slices from gear to gear.

A newcomer to Alfas may find the Giulietta initially disappointing, all the same. The clutch appears sudden, the steering is heavy at low speed, and the brakes demand a fair effort. But drop a gear – to get the most out of the car, you need to use the gearbox to the full – and the little saloon comes alive. The steering lightens, and you can revel in its perfect weighting and precision; the clutch reveals itself as light and instant, and the brakes offer progressive and reassuring retardation.

Roadholding, thanks to the careful suspension design, is safe and predictable. Increasing power on the way into a bend tends to accentuate the natural degree of initial understeer. Oversteer can be provoked at the outset by insensitive drivers, but loading the rear of the car with passengers and luggage helps to emphasise the design's natural stability.

At first the handling seems unpromising, with large amounts of body roll on entering a corner. But that initial roll is all you get: once the car is set up for a corner it scuttles round with impressive security. Thanks to the sensitive and lively feel through the wheel, and the taut but far from harsh suspension, you can hustle the Giulietta with genuine confidence – helped by the commanding driving position.

On a familiar cross-country journey you end up averaging a higher speed, taking less time, and seemingly expending less effort. In its performance and its responsiveness the Alfa strikes a delicious balance between all the desirable virtues of a sporting saloon: it demands to be driven fast, and rewards you substantially for your efforts.

Buying Hints

1. All the conventional rust points apply on the Berlina – sills, wheelarches, wing bottoms, floors (in extremis), and behind the headlamps. Localised patching or fabricating sections from scratch will be the only solution: panels are near unobtainable and repair sections are not available.

2. The front and central chassis outriggers can rot; refabrication from scratch is the only answer, so the work will be expensive. This applies to the Spider and Sprint as well as the Berlina.

3. Under the front wheelarches on Giulietta Berlinas – and on Giulietta/Giulia Sprints and Spiders – there is a curved-section bracing member running from the bulkhead to the upper mounting for the spring. Road dirt enters this member and rots it. If this has led to corrosion of the inner wing this may be visible in the engine bay.

4. Rust can take hold around the mounting points for the steering box and the steering idler; again, this applies to the Sprint/Spider as well as to the Berlina.

5. Brightwork is near unobtainable, so beware cars that are incomplete or badly below par in this respect.

6. The engine is robust and long-lived, although over-exuberance can cause burnt-out exhaust valves; on 101 series cars this can be avoided in the future by fitting sodium-filled valves from a 105 series Giulia. Timing-chain rattle is to be expected, but changing chains is not too difficult. Head gaskets are prone to blow if the car has not been allowed to warm up before being taken out: look for traces of oil at the block-to-head join, and oil in the water. This applies to all Alfa twin-cam engines, and if left to worsen can result in a warped head. Gasket and head problems can also be provoked by corrosion – exacerbated by poor anti-freeze – causing the steel cylinder liners to sink. Water pumps are no more vulnerable than on any car: a rattle from the bearings indicates imminent trouble.

7. Be aware that many survivors have been up-engined with 1570cc units, as likely as not with five-speed floor-change gearboxes. By all means try to bargain a lower price on grounds of non-originality, but be content that in everyday use you'll have a better car.

8. On all post-war classic Alfa engines Golden Lodge sparking plugs should be used; the use of incorrect plugs is not a good sign, as these could provoke holed pistons.

9. The 750 series Giuliettas made up until 1959 have a less strong gearbox with inferior synchromesh. Subsequent (101 series) cars have an improved version of the 1900 box, with Porsche-type synchromesh, and this unit is used on all subsequent front-gearbox Alfas; it is a robust item and the only problem you are typically likely to encounter is slow synchromesh on second, an ailment generally caused by unsympathetic handling before the oil has warmed up. The only other problem you may come across is jumping out of reverse gear under load, as a result of a bent selector fork. Consider a 750-series Giulietta fitted with a 101 series gearbox as being enhanced rather than debased by this modification.

10. The stub axles pivot on balljoints on all Alfas from the Giulietta onwards; checking for wear demands a bit of high-energy levering, but parts are readily available. As ever, the rubber gaiters can split.

11. The rear axle is immensely strong. It will suffer from leaks, especially if the car has stood, allowing the oil seals to dry and harden; rear suspension bushes wear, leading to sloppy handling.

12. All front-gearbox Alfas of the post-war generation have a split propshaft. The rubber support for the central bearing tends to fail, and the rubber doughnut coupling at the gearbox end is prone to splitting; a visual check will reveal both maladies.

13. The brake-pedal assembly on right-hand-drive Giuliettas and their derivatives is half outside the pedal box, and if the protective shield is missing it is exposed to road dirt. This can cause the pedal to seize on its shaft, preventing it from returning. A period dealer's tweak was to fit a grease nipple between the clutch and brake pedals.

14. Steering idlers tend to be worn, and in need of re-bushing. Rock the road wheel on the side in question and see if there is movement of the curved steering arm dropping down from the idler. The steering box lasts well, although you should check all the same for excessive slop in the system; roughness could indicate that water has got into the system and caused corrosion.

Alfa Romeo *Giulia*

By the early 1960s it was clear that the Giulietta was being overtaken by competitors with bigger engines, greater power and higher performance. Equally, in view of the Giulietta's direct descent from its 1900 predecessor, it was also apparent that the engine design, the chassis and the suspension would certainly benefit from uprating without the need for too much fundamental modification.

This was the rationale behind the Giulia, which made its first appearance at a press launch held at the Monza racing circuit on 27 June 1962. This time there was no need for a lottery or a Bertone-bodied stopgap to save the day, so one of the first three models to appear was a basic saloon, albeit with a far from basic specification.

The uncompromisingly boxy style of the Giulia TI in its earliest form. (Alfa Romeo archives)

This was the Giulia TI, which caused something of a sensation in that its styling owed far less to the Giulietta saloon than that had to the 1900. Gone was all hint of a family resemblance, apart from the radiator grille and the badge. The Giulia saloon was a much more literal rendition of the 'three-box' theme than usual, with square-cut lines that made it stand out from virtually all its competitors.

Designed like its two post-war predecessors by Dr Orazio Satta Puliga, the priorities of the Giulia

With the Giulia range Alfa became volume producers of sporting-style thoroughbreds

bodyshape were twofold: to offer as much space as possible for people, luggage and mechanicals within its still fairly compact dimensions, and to do so with as much aerodynamic efficiency as possible. The rectilinear styling answered the first requirement, with the added bonus that it was

With the arrival in 1962 of the Giulia, Alfa was offering three ranges, and a choice of seven body styles. Back row (left to right) are the 2600 Sprint, Giulietta Berlina, 2600 Berlina and 101-series Sprint, with the front row comprising (left to right) the new Giulia, the 101-series Spider, and the 2600 Spider. (Alfa Romeo archives)

relatively simple to produce. What was more surprising was how careful detailing gave such an unpromising shape an encouragingly low drag coefficient. Thanks to features proved in wind-tunnel testing, such as the sharply descending bonnet line to part the airflow on entry, and the sharply cut-off Kamm tail to minimise turbulence at the rear, the car was well placed to put any extra power output to full use.

This was just as well, because the other major change was an increase in engine size. By enlarging the bores by 4mm and lengthening the stroke by 7mm, Alfa's design team revived the proportions of the old 1900 engine in a smaller size, after the almost 'square' dimensions of the Giulietta. Capacity was now 1570cc, but as with the Giulietta the combustion chamber shape was a

Giulia TI
1962–1968
ENGINE:
Four-cylinder, twin ohc
Bore x stroke	78 x 82mm
Capacity	1,570cc
Power	92bhp

TRANSMISSION:
Five-speed gearbox
Final drive:	5.125:1

BODY STYLE:
Four-door saloon

PERFORMANCE:
(from contemporary sources)
Max speed	103mph (165kph)
0–60mph (97kph)	13.3 seconds

LENGTH:	13ft 7in (4.14m)
WIDTH:	5ft 1.4in (1.56m)
WHEELBASE:	8ft 3in (2.51m)

Giulia Super
1964–1978
As Giulia TI, except:
Power	98–102bhp
Final drive:	4.556:1

PERFORMANCE:
(from contemporary sources)
Max speed	109mph (175kph)
0–60mph (97kph)	11.4 seconds

NUMBER BUILT:
Giulia 1300	325,844
Giulia TI	71,148
Giulia Super	177,897
Giulia TI Super	501

Always a favourite with the Italian police, the Giulia TI was a popular rapid-response vehicle. (Alfa Romeo archives)

flattened version of the true hemispherical sections used on earlier Alfa engines, to allow for larger valves.

This produced a slightly taller engine, which had to be canted over to the left to fit beneath the lower bonnet. The better breathing resulting from larger valves was combined with a 9:1 compression ratio and a double-choke Weber carburettor to produce a power output of 92bhp. The car was slightly heavier, at a dry weight of nearly 20cwt, thanks largely to a more luxurious and comfortable interior, but performance was nonetheless improved by a substantial margin. Top speed increased to 103mph (166kph), and acceleration was improved all the way up the range, aided by a five-speed gearbox, albeit one still controlled through a complex steering-column change. In recognition of the new body, the

Giulia model numbers had a '105' prefix instead of the '101' of the later Giuliettas. The only exceptions were the Sprints and Spiders (see Chapter 4), which were simply re-engined Giuliettas.

Roadholding was improved. The spring settings and suspension geometry still encouraged a degree of body roll, but the tendency to disconcerting sideways hops was now eliminated. The solution was not to change the location system for the rear axle, but to replace the old triangular frame with a T-shaped piece of forged steel that provided a much firmer anchorage against unwanted lateral movement. The character and performance of the car were a definite improvement on earlier models, and with the Giulia range the company was at last to establish its reputation as a successful volume producer of sporting-character thoroughbreds.

The Giulia TI and its stablemates were to break new ground in two other ways, both increasingly important for the company's commercial success. More of them were to be made and sold than any earlier model, and more were to be exported to increasingly hungry overseas markets. So far as British motorists were concerned, the big news was the introduction of a right-hand-drive version of the Giulia from November 1962, backed by the replacement of Thomson & Taylor, who had served as Alfa Romeo importers for almost 30 years, by Alfa Romeo's own UK subsidiary, Alfa Romeo (Great Britain) Limited.

Variants on the Giulia appeared thick and fast. First came a limited production sporting version of the TI, designated the Giulia TI Super, and of

which only 501 would be made. It was announced in April 1963 and deleted a year later. The TI Super was fitted with disc brakes all round, possibly apart from the very first cars, as were regular TIs after the first 22,000 to emerge from the factory, and all subsequent models in the Giulia range. With a 9.7:1 compression ratio, sharper cam settings and twin double-choke Webers, engine power rose to 112bhp at 6500rpm, and low-speed torque was considerably increased. Not only did this quicken acceleration and raise the top speed to 115mph (184kph), but thanks to the fitting of individual bucket seats at the front rather than the bench of the 1900, Giulietta and original Giulia TI, comfort when exploiting this power was greatly improved.

Other additions increased driver appeal. The substitution of a large circular speedometer for the old

The Giulia Super: similar from the outside, although a great deal more sporty on the inside. (Alfa Romeo archives)

The smaller-engined Giulias

Alfa-minded customers suffering from taxation-by-engine-capacity, as was the case in Italy, had the option of choosing a smaller-engined version. This appeared as the Giulia 1300, launched at Monza on 11 May 1964. In spite of the name, it made use of the already popular and well-proven Giulietta TI engine, fitted into a less-embellished Giulia TI body.

The 1300 had a four-speed gearbox and a strip speedometer at first, just as the original Giulia TI, but was fitted with a floor gearchange and bucket seats at the front. From 1968 the car had a revised dashboard layout with circular instruments. The power peak was raised to 78bhp at 6,000rpm, and in spite of an increase in weight over the Giulietta TI, it had a virtually identical performance, with a top speed of 96mph (155kph). It was remarkably successful as an addition to the range, with 28,358 having been

made by 1971, when the model was discontinued. However, its appeal was more limited outside Italy, and these cars were rare in overseas markets.

More successful altogether was the TI version of the Giulia 1300, which was launched on 4 February 1966. This had a much more lavishly equipped interior on the lines of the bigger engined cars, and had a 9:1 compression ratio, a five-speed gearbox with a floor change, bucket front seats and a top speed of 100mph (160kph). On the home market the TI sold for less than three-fifths the price of the Giulia Super, and was to prove one of the most successful of all the Giulia saloons, over six years of production. A total of 144,213 were made, and this included 2,860 right-hand-drive versions destined for overseas markets.

RIGHT:
The later Giulia Nuova Super 1300 of 1974 onwards had the plastic grille and wider radiator shield of the later Giulias, and the four-headlamp installation of the original Giulia TI; the hubcaps have been replaced by nave plates. (Alfa Romeo archives)

From 1970 the Giulia 1300 and 1300 TI were joined by a better-equipped Giulia 1300 Super, which ultimately replaced them. In facelifted Nuova Super 1300 form, introduced in 1974, the model lasted until 1978.

The Giulia 1300 TI is identifiable from the front by a single pair of headlamps, rather than the double pair of the 1600 Giulias. (LAT)

A late Giulia interior with a dished steering wheel and the gear lever in a central console, as in the 1750 and 2000 saloons. (LAT)

linear-strip instrument, and the change from a column shift to a neat floor-mounted change, gently spring-biased towards the third–fourth plane, made the TI Super even more enjoyable to drive quickly. A new three-spoke steering wheel was fitted, and there were light alloy road wheels, while Alfa Corse four-leaf clover badges on the sides and rear reminded customers of the car's sporting potential and matchless heritage.

In between the TI and the TI Super, Alfa Romeo slotted the Giulia Super saloon, this appearing at the Geneva Motor Show in 1965. The newcomer had twin double-choke carburettors, a 9:1 compression ratio, and a peak power output of 98bhp at 5500rpm. To relieve the still rather utilitarian lines of the body, Alfa also introduced some discreet embellishments, with a longitudinal chrome strip running on the sills, revised rear light clusters,

and a small metal four-leaf clover on the rear quarter window pillar.

The original Giulia TI stayed in production for five years, and in all 71,148 were made, with just under one-third of them fitted with the floor-mounted gearchange that became optional from 1964. Of this total, just 1412 were made in right-hand-drive form. However the TI was to be totally eclipsed, in commercial terms, by the Giulia Super, which stayed in the company catalogue from 1965 to 1978, with a total production of 177,897 units, excluding 6,572 diesel versions.

In 1971, the Super was given a series of improvements including a floor-mounted handbrake to replace the dashboard-mounted version, twin brake circuits, top-hinged pedals, warning lights for brake fluid level and handbrake operation, and power output up to 102bhp, together with a more luxurious interior with additional instruments. Facelifted in 1974 to become the Nuova Super 1600 (New Super 1600), manufacture continued until 1978, with a diesel-engined version available from 1976.

With more power and performance, improved handling and unmistakable lines that set them apart from their closest competitors, the Giulia saloons won over a wealth of new customers from outside the ranks of traditional Alfa Romeo enthusiasts. The Giulia has a close family resemblance to the familar Giulietta. The bigger engine gives more performance and greater flexibility, and the extra ratio in the gearbox provides better means to exploit the power on offer. Later cars with more lavish appointments and a full

complement of round dials add to the appeal, and a '67 Giulia Super is one of the author's favourites, being more welcoming inside, blessed with a fraction more power than the TI and having an added dose of responsiveness.

With the Giulias there is still that characteristic Alfa roll, but the car grips and grips, and with its responsive steering is delightfully chuckable. The brakes (whether drum or disc) demand a good lean, the ride is lively, and the rear end can hop about on poor surfaces, but with that hard-edged and rev-happy twin-cam and that splendidly fluid spring-loaded five-speed floor change, who would really want to complain?

With a surprising quietness for the

Side view of a 1970 Giulia Super: its square-cut lines were in fact surprisingly efficient aerodynamically. (LAT)

In its final form, the Nuova Giulia Super, the Giulia was available with 1300 or 1600 power, or – from June 1976 – with a 1760cc Perkins four-cylinder diesel developing 52bhp DIN. (Alfa Romeo archives)

The magazine found that the improvements that had been made to the Giulietta suspension had earned their keep: '. . .a drive in the TI demonstrates dramatically just how effective a properly done live axle rear end can be. It stays on the road, shows no tendency to hop on hard acceleration and little propensity for juddering in a rough bend.' Even though the test car still had drum brakes all round, the writer had no complaints, and the brakes 'were fully up to whatever was asked of them'.

Three years later *Road and Track* tested the Giulia Super, and once again found it no beauty, but with well-nigh impeccable road manners. 'It's nothing much in the way of pretty, what with slab sides and boxy lines, but it sure is everything else a car of this type ought to be. If you're under the hood, attached to the gearshift lever, holding the steering wheel or motoring down the road it says Alfa, Alfa, Alfa – and that's a pretty nice thing to say to any enthusiastic motorist.'

time, thanks to those efficient aerodynamics, the Giulia is the perfect car for the family man who wants to cover long distances on B roads and emerge with a smile on his face. Nor need he feel short-changed if all he can find is a 1300-engined Giulia: what these junior Giulias lack in outright 'go' they make up for in their well-mannered sweetness. No wonder some Alfisti prefer them to their bigger-engined siblings.

The American journal *Road and Track* tested a Giulia TI in 1965, and was slow to warm to its looks, which the writer described as 'boxy, square at all corners and [with] more of the looks of one of the workaday medium-size Fiats than the sleek sexiness we ordinarily expect attached to the Alfa emblem.' He went on to admit that 'underneath that unprepossessing exterior, however, there is as fine a set of 1600 internals as you'll find anywhere.'

After praising the brakes, the handling and the gearbox, the magazine managed to find fault with the driving position, which, as with all Alfas of the time, is designed for Italian rather than Anglo-Saxon combinations of height and leg length. Other gripes centred on engine vibration, poor heating and ventilation (highlighting the heater indicator light – 'a very practical accessory because otherwise you'd probably never be able to tell whether the heater was on or not') and single-speed windscreen wipers. But what the American testers said about the Giulia's performance was particularly appropriate. They felt that the Giulia Super showed that 'no compact sedan really needs to have anything bigger than a 2-liter engine'. And that, strangely enough, was what Alfa Romeo had in mind for the Giulia – in time.

Buying Hints

1. The Giulia 105s are less well made than the earlier saloons and suffer from the poorer-quality steel used in their construction; expect therefore to inspect some heart-sinkingly miserable examples.

2. The outer sills rot, as do the inner bracing panels; if caught in time, however, this sill corrosion need not have spread to the join between the inner sill and the floor.

3. The footwells rust by the front jacking points and the floor can hole by the front seat mountings; the rear footwells can fray around their large circular drainholes.

4. The rear wheelarches, rear valance (which is a box section) and the rear door shuts are prone to corrosion; repair sections are available for the rear arches and the rear valance. Still at the rear, rust can set in at the seam of the rear panel, leading to perforation, while the bootlid bottom can also rust badly.

5. A substantial return to the panelwork around the headlamps is a natural rust-trap; the back of the front wings also corrodes, as – predictably enough – do the door bottoms.

6. Common to 105-series Giulia Berlinas and the related Bertone coupés and Pininfarina Duetto/Spider models is corrosion of the crossmember under the radiator.

7. The bright embellisher around the door windows can provoke corrosion of the window sill area, while the door-mirror fixing can generate further rot.

8. Mechanical checkpoints are generally as for the preceding Alfa models, but note that servos and master-cylinders for cars with twin-circuit brakes are no longer available.

9. Squeaks from the front suspension over bumps may indicate worn Silentbloc bushes; these are not easy to replace. At the rear, similar noises may be solved merely by lubricating the pivots of the A-bracket locating the axle; if this doesn't do the trick, the bushes are likely to be shot. These points apply to all front-gearbox Alfas from the 105 Giulia series onwards.

10. The front spring pans can rot away, and replacement demands caution and – ideally – a special tool. This applies also to the 105-derived coupés, the 1750/2000 Berlinas, and the Spiders. At the rear, sagging springs are not unusual.

11. Don't feel that a car with three-shoe front drum brakes is inferior to a disc-braked car: the former brakes are massively engineered and provide strong stopping power. Refurbishing a triple-shoe set-up is not cheap, however; nor is their adjustment easy. Beware, therefore, of such cars (including 101-series Giulias) with out-of-sorts braking.

12. As engines on Alfas became more powerful, so greater stresses were placed on the engine mounts. Check therefore for engine mountings that have sheared: rock the engine vigorously. Look out also for cracked exhaust manifolds.

13. The rubber carburettor mounts can harden and split, causing air leaks. A hissing suggests air leaks: if in doubt, spray WD40 on the mounts with the engine running, and the revs should rise if there is a leak.

14. The correct material for the interior trim is available from an American specialist.

Giulietta & Giulia
Sprints & Spiders

If the Giulietta and Giulia saloons were following the lead of the 1900 in providing Alfas that looked ordinary enough while delivering surprisingly good performance, their success paved the way for a series of variations on the basic theme that lived up to the company's glorious heritage by looking every bit as good as their performance merited. Because of the delays in starting production of Giulietta saloon bodies in the run-up to the launch in 1954, and the problems with the lottery organised to help finance the project,

This side view of a Sprint – a late 1300 – shows its clean aerodynamic profile. (Alfa Romeo archives)

a desperate Alfa Romeo, as we have already seen, commissioned Bertone to produce a small series of coupés in order to have something to show the press and to give away as prizes, before the mass-production saloon was ready.

This definite placing of the cart before the horse was about the only way out of the company's problems, since only the skill, speed and flexibility of the teams of craftsmen working for a classic coachbuilder could produce results in time. Even

so, it was an extraordinary achievement. The basis for the car was a pair of 'mules' (*muletti*) built in the factory for testing the engine, components and running gear of the new model. In the autumn of 1953 one was given to Bertone and the other to Boano, of Carrozzeria Ghia. Rudolf Hruska, an Austrian engineer who had moved to Alfa from Porsche to become the company's Technical Manager, invited the companies to quote for a prototype for the company stand at the Turin Show in the spring of 1954, and for a small production run of up to 1000 vehicles.

Boano's design was the more ambitious, and Ghia had the resources to produce the necessary cars quickly. Bertone, on the other hand, used the rough proportions of the 'mule' to create an elegant and balanced shape that in the event would go on to serve Alfa well for more than a decade. This was the design that Hruska chose, but Bertone's limited production facilities

Bertone would now have to produce all the cars in his own tiny workshop

would not be able to meet the likely demand. The eventual solution was an Italian compromise – Bertone would make the prototype, and Ghia would make the production versions. Then Boano and Ghia fell out, lawsuits were fired in all directions, and the whole agreement came unglued.

This meant that Bertone would have to produce all the cars in his own tiny workshop. The original prototype had progressed from a wooden mock-up to a hand-finished body, with a radiator grille borrowed from the then new Romeo panel delivery van. It duly appeared on the company stand at the Turin Show, and the public loved

Giulietta Sprint/Sprint Veloce
1954–1962

ENGINE:
Four-cylinder, twin ohc

Bore x stroke	74 x 75mm
Capacity	1290cc
Power	80bhp
	(Veloce 90bhp)

TRANSMISSION:
Four-speed gearbox

Final drive	4.555:1
	(Veloce 4.1)

BODY STYLE:
Two-door coupé

PERFORMANCE:
(from contemporary sources)

Max speed	103mph (165kph)
Veloce	112mph (180kph)
0–60mph (97kph)	14.8 seconds
Veloce	14.2 seconds

LENGTH:	13ft 2in (4.01m)
WIDTH:	5ft 2in (1.57m)
WHEELBASE:	7ft 10in (2.38m)

Giulia 1600 Sprint
1962–64

As Giulietta Sprint except:

Power	92bhp
Max speed	107mph (172kph)
0–60mph (97kph)	13.2 seconds

Giulietta Spider/Spider Veloce
1955–62

As Giulietta Sprint except:

BODY STYLE:	Two-seat roadster
LENGTH:	12ft 9.5in (3.89m)
WIDTH:	5ft 2.2in (1.58m)
WHEELBASE:	7ft 4.6in (2.25m)

Giulia 1600 Spider/Spider Veloce
1962–65

As Giulietta Spider except:

Power	92bhp
	(Veloce 112bhp)
Max speed	107mph (172kph)
Veloce more than 112mph (180kph)	

Giulietta SS
1957–62

As Giulietta Sprint except:

Power	100bhp
Max Speed	122mph (200kph)
0–60mph (97kph)	12.4 seconds

LENGTH:	13ft 11in (4.24m)
WIDTH:	5ft 5.3in (1.66m)
WHEELBASE:	7ft 4in (2.25m)

Giulia SS
1963–66

As Giulietta SS except:

Power	112bhp
Max speed	122mph (200kph)
0–60mph (97kph)	12.0 seconds

NUMBER BUILT:

Giulietta Sprint	24,084
Giulietta Sprint Veloce	3,058
Giulia 1600 Sprint	7,107
1300 Sprint	1,900
Giulietta Spider	14,300
Giulietta Spider Veloce	2,796
Giulia 1600 Spider	9,250
Giulia 1600 Spider Veloce	1,091
Giulietta SS	1,366
Giulia SS	1,400

The Giulietta Sprint began life as a clever adaptation by Bertone of the factory 'mules' used for testing the mechanical assemblies while the saloon body/chassis unit was still under development; note the simple style of side air intake originally used, and the tailgate found only on the 'lottery' cars. (Alfa Romeo archives)

technical sinew to turn out more of the sleek little coupés. Five years after the appearance of the prototype, output had increased from four bodies a day to 34. The completed bodies were taken to the Alfa Romeo works at Portello for the mechanical parts to be fitted on a production line. In the meantime, the original order for 1000 cars had been increased to 6,000, and by the time the Giulietta Sprint was phased out in 1962, a total of more than 27,000 had been made. Its replacement, the Giulia Sprint, would use the same body for another 7,107 cars.

What did the buyers receive for their money? For a price 26 per cent more than that of the Giulietta Berlina (when it finally appeared), they had a sleek 2+2 closed coupé with a fastback roofline curving down to the rear in a style that suggested speed and performance; on the first batch of cars there was a lift-up tailgate, but this soon gave way to a conventional bootlid. The Giulietta engine was given a higher 8.5:1 compression ratio and initially a single twin-choke carburettor, resulting in 80bhp at 6,300rpm. Although the chassis was the same as the saloon, Bertone's coupé was actually 77lb (35kg) lighter, and its top speed was a healthy 103mph (165kph).

In other mechanical respects the cars were virtually identical at the start. Early Sprints were fitted with a four-speed gearbox, and the first 7,300 cars retained the steering-column gearchange. With a hard-working 1.3-litre engine this meant a fairly noisy interior, but the appointments were more luxurious than for the saloon, and the car's appearance made up for a great deal. Much of its appeal, now as then, lies in the combination of its virtues adding up to a thoroughly well-balanced whole, with a responsiveness and performance truly outstanding for a relatively small-engined coupé of the mid-1950s.

it. It was clear that every one of the planned production versions – to be called the Sprint – could have been sold several times over, and eight weeks after the show Alfa pressed Bertone to double his output. At the time it seemed impossible, yet demand and production grew side by side.

Bertone switched from wooden formers to steel dies, built a vast new workshop, took on more workers and strained every commercial and

The interior of a Giulietta Sprint, as depicted in an Alfa brochure. (Peter Marshall collection)

If the Giulietta Sprint represented a return, in a more modern idiom, to the kind of Alfa Romeo that had been offered to pre-war customers, the next variation marked a further progression. This was another coachbuilt design, but by Pininfarina rather than Bertone. By shortening the wheelbase by 5 inches (13cm), but keeping the front and rear track the same, the chassis was able to carry a neat two-seater open roadster body, and save 44lb (20kg) in weight.

The Giulietta Spider appeared in the summer of 1955. It became an instant classic and proved almost as much of a success in production terms as the Sprint coupé: in seven years just over 17,000 were made. It had the same engine as the Sprint, and the same top speed, but the combination of almost ageless styling and an easily opened hood in a genuine sports two-seater matched the company badge on the bonnet more closely even than its two stablemates. It was marginally more expensive than the Sprint, and 38 per cent more expensive than the saloon, but it

seemed to belong in a different league altogether.

As with the Sprint, the detail finish on the Spider was so good as to excite comment. Not only were the engine head and block cast in light alloy, initially with crackle-finished cam boxes, but the ribbed sump and transmission housing were cast in aluminium, as was the final drive housing. The front brake drums were cast in light alloy around a ferrous lining, and incorporated deeply machined diagonal ribs to increase

the cooling surface area and direct the airflow over the hottest part of the drum.

Inside the car the instruments were laid out in a compact cluster behind the steering wheel and directly in the driver's line of sight. In the centre was a large circular tachometer, flanked by a circular speedometer and a cluster of instruments showing fuel tank contents, water temperature and oil temperature. Two bucket seats provided plenty of grip even in sharp cornering, and a moderately long gearlever curved upwards and backwards from below the dashboard.

The public reaction to the car's first appearance was one of barely suppressed enthusiasm. By 1959 the original 750 series engines had been replaced by the tougher 101 series power units, as already mentioned, and other changes included a wheelbase lengthened by 2 inches (5cm) on the Spider. The Spider also gained quarter lights, and the Sprint a modified grille and hinged rear side windows instead of fixed panes. The American journal *Road and Track* had

A well-preserved Dutch-registered Sprint. (LAT)

The purposeful prow of the Giulietta Spider: it never received the fussier front end of later Sprints. (LAT)

tested the Spider three years earlier, soon after its introduction, and had no hesitation in describing it as 'the most fascinating small sports car we have ever driven'.

Features singled out for particular praise included the handling. *Road and Track* commented that 'the adhesion to the road is absolutely uncanny. In cornering there is moderate understeer, very light caster-pull on the steering wheel rim, no noticeable body roll and no squealing from the Pirelli tyres until the absolute limit of adhesion has been exceeded.' Brakes, too, came in for high marks. 'Second only to the impeccable handling and roadability of the Giulietta must come the brakes which are close to if not absolutely the best we have ever experienced . . . the bi-metallic drums have a most impressive look too, with 72 massive

The Giulietta Spider became the classic post-war Alfa roadster, thanks to its compact lines and brisk performance; the lack of quarterlights identifies this car as a 750-series Spider with the shorter wheelbase. (LAT)

cooling fins per drum placed at an angle for positive air circulation. There's no fade here.'

The car was also praised for the fitting of wind-up windows, although most people found that the large number of turns required spoiled the pleasure slightly. All the same they were a great improvement on flapping sidescreens or sliding windows, and in this respect set the trend for future sports cars. The only other criticisms concerned the driving position for short drivers (who had to peer beneath the steering wheel rim) and tall ones (who found their heads brushing the roof), while the 'feeble' horn was quite lost in the noise of heavy traffic.

From the time of their introduction, both the Sprint and Spider provided an exhilarating combination of character and performance, within the limits of what was possible even with a well-designed 1.3-litre engine. However, as with pre-war Alfa Romeos, the dealers were soon pestering the factory for an uprated version for buyers with competition in mind. In 1956 the Giulietta Sprint and Spider Veloces duly appeared, with uprated engines and modified bodywork.

High-crown pistons raised the compression ratio to 9.1:1, which with a pair of double-choke carburettors and more peaky cam profiles raised power to 90bhp at 6,500rpm. The Sprint was fitted with Perspex sliding windows, and the door panels that enclosed the winding mechanism on the standard car were hollowed out to provide more elbow room. In addition the fuel tank was increased in capacity from the standard 11.7 gallons (53 litres) to 17.6 gallons (80 litres) to provide extra range and cope with the increased thirst. The Spider, where room was restricted, had to be content with the original tankage.

Other changes to the Spider included bonnet, bootlid and doors in

aluminium alloy to save weight. Both versions had aluminium bumpers, yet in spite of these careful modifications the weight of the cars actually increased – by 11lb (5kg) for the Spider and by 33lb (15kg) for the Sprint. Nevertheless, performance was certainly improved. Top speed climbed to 112mph (180kph), and the 0–60mph time was cut from 15 seconds to 13 seconds, while responsiveness was improved all the way up the range.

All these different versions of the Giulietta proved one fact above all, that the little Giulietta engine worked wonders in delivering power and performance totally out of keeping for a 1.3-litre unit. Great things were

Most Spiders, like most Alfas, were painted Italian racing red, but the second most popular colour was white. This is a pre-production model with a panoramic screen and sliding sidescreens: when manufacture began the screen was flatter and there were winding windows. (Alfa Romeo archives)

The 1570cc version of the Alfa twin-cam four-cylinder engine fits snugly under the compact bonnet of this 1964 Giulia Spider. (LAT)

had engines with a 9:1 compression ratio, delivering 92bhp at 6,200rpm and providing a top speed of 107mph (172kph).

In the two years 1962–64, 7,107 Giulia Sprints were made, with the last 107 switching at last from the big-finned drum brakes to discs at the front. This time there was no Veloce version for those willing to pay a little more for extra performance, but this choice was still available for buyers of the Spider, which continued in production for another year. This version had the compression ratio raised to 9.7:1 and a pair of double-choke carburettors, boosting power to 112bhp at 6,500 rpm. The top speed went up to more than 112mph (180kph), and the car became one of the all-time Alfa classics. Where the Giulietta Spider had produced surprising performance for such a small-engined car, the Giulia Spider Veloce could compete in all but the biggest and most powerful company.

The Giulia Spider proved even more successful than the Giulia Sprint. In three years 9,250 were made, with another 1,091 of the Veloce version. *Road and Track* tested one in September 1965 and loved the performance, the 'superb' gearbox, and as always the handling. There were a few criticisms, including the poor view over the rear quarters with the hood in place and the restricted width of the seats (at least for one heavily built member of the test team). But the magazine's final verdict must have been exactly what its makers longed to hear. 'All things considered', it said, 'the Alfa Romeo 1600 [Spider] Veloce is an excellent sports car by any standards: its responsiveness, accurate handling and ease of operation make it a continuing pleasure for either the skilled driver or the novice, and it undoubtedly has all those intangible personality factors which have always enabled Alfas to form close, rewarding relationships with their owners.'

While the bigger-engined Giulia Sprints and Spiders were continuing to delight, those with less deep pockets were catered for by the re-introduction, in 1963, of a 1290cc Sprint. Effectively reviving the former Giulietta Sprint, the model was called the 1300 Sprint and was offered until 1965; in all 1900 were made.

The glowing remarks of the period press ring as true today as they did then, with the 750 series and 101 series coupé and Spider building on the recipe familiar from the Giulietta saloon. The direct and incisive steering and gearchange, revvy engines and balanced handling are all as you might predict. These are not out-and-out fast motor cars, but they

Driver's eye view of the Giulia Spider, with instruments behind the steering wheel, short gear lever and bucket seats providing traditional sports-car appeal. (LAT)

therefore expected when the larger-bore, longer-stroke 1570cc version appeared in the new Giulia saloon, and in 1962 the Giulietta Sprint and Spider inherited the new 1.6 litre engine to become the Giulia 1600 Sprint and Giulia 1600 Spider respectively. In spite of the larger engine the power increase was initially modest, but what really counted was the boost in low-down torque: when the cars were fitted with the five-speed gearbox introduced on the Sprint Zagato and Sprint Speciale, the performance and flexibility of the cars was really transformed. In their original specification, the re-named models

A 1570cc Giulia Sprint models the revised frontal treatment introduced with the 101-series Sprint in 1959. (Alfa Romeo archives)

have a brio and an immediacy that makes them involving – intoxicating, even – to drive on a favourite country road.

A good test of any car's sporting credentials is its steering, and these Alfas have a quickness of response and a communicativeness that prove that a rack is not obligatory in a sports car. There is still a dose of the Giulietta's roll, but the roadholding is as tenacious as you have a right to expect. Take it easy, furthermore, and you'll be surprised by the flexibility and tractability of the engine – most particularly in the case of the 1570cc cars.

Comparisons with British sports cars of the era are instructive. While you might enjoy the crisp fail-safe competence of an MGA's chassis, with the MG's pushrod engine you will not have the carved-from-the-solid urgency of Alfa's twin-cams; if, on the other hand, you find a Big Healey's lazy torque seductive, you'll have to put up with a ponderous gearchange and demandingly primitive road manners, in contrast to the poise and delicacy of the Italian cars. That's the Alfa difference.

The Giulietta SZ and SS ... and Giulia SS

Both the Sprint and the Spider, in standard and Veloce versions, made full use of the splendid Giulietta mechanical set-up to provide character and performance in a small and relatively economical package. However, the models that really showed the capabilities of the design were two more special versions produced in smaller numbers, and today greatly popular with collectors. One was built with competition in mind by Carrozzeria Zagato, builders of the splendid sports and racing 1750 and 2300 pre-war Alfa Romeos, and the other was a more extravagantly shaped version by Bertone.

This front view of the Giulietta SZ (Sprint Zagato) shows how the frontal area was reduced and aerodynamic efficiency improved. (Alfa Romeo archives)

The Giulietta Sprint SZ (for Sprint Zagato) was the more purposeful of the two. It appeared as a prototype in 1957, with series production beginning in 1960, and used the same

The earlier Giulietta SZs had a rounded tail that owed more to styling than to aerodynamic testing. (LAT)

floorpan and running gear as the Sprint and Spider, but overbuilt with the usual Zagato spaceframe of square-section small-bore steel tubes, clothed with carefully shaped light-alloy panels. As with its pre-war predecessor, the 1750, the Sprint SZ was designed for function rather than style. The unassuming body shape was very efficient aerodynamically, with a low frontal area and a minimum of drag-inducing details.

Great care was taken to reduce weight as far as possible. Apart from the light-alloy panelling, the side windows were made from Perspex rather than glass, and at its introduction the SZ weighed a mere 15.5cwt. (785kg). Although the interior was relatively spartan, with rubber mats rather than carpets, an almost total absence of crash padding, and no sunvisors, the SZ did provide a pair of solid bucket seats with wrap-around sides; however, the pretence at rear passenger room of

The inside of this Giulietta Kamm-tail SZ is luxurious by competition standards, but the wrap-around seats and the layout of the instruments betray the sporting origins of the design. (LAT)

Sprint Speciale, or SS, first seen as a prototype in 1957, represented style and craftsmanship. The ordinary Giulietta Sprint had been the car that Bertone *had* to build, because its design needed to be based closely on the factory mules and work was against the clock to produce a design that could be shown, and sold, to the public. The Sprint Speciale, on the other hand, was the car he *wanted* to build, where elegance went hand-in-hand with improved aerodynamic efficiency.

As the Giulietta SZ, the SS had originally been intended as a potential racer, with plastic windows and alloy body panels. But before the first production versions emerged in 1959, the decision was taken to build the SS as a properly-appointed road car, as a GT coupé with the looks and

The SZ was a very practical proposition as a long-distance roadgoing GT car

the ordinary Sprint was reduced to a mere luggage platform.

Thanks to a higher compression ratio of 9.7:1 and two double-choke horizontal carburettors, the Giulietta engine was persuaded to deliver a resounding 100bhp at 6,500rpm. Driving through a five-speed gearbox, this delivered a 0–60mph time of just over 11 seconds and an all-out top speed of more than 120mph (200kph). When the American journal *Road and Track* tested an SZ in December 1961 it was happy to pronounce it 'one of the best cars we've ever driven'. Certainly in the dry the handling was superb, and the big drum brakes usually coped well in

hard use with a minimum of fade. In wet conditions, however, some drivers reported that the short wheelbase and high power-to-weight ratio made it easy to provoke a slide.

For out-and-out racing use, the Giulietta SZ could be ordered with an engine tuned by Conrero delivering 115bhp. This allowed a top speed of more than 125mph (200kph). The last 30 Giulietta SZs appeared in 1962, after exhaustive wind-tunnel testing, with a lower roofline and a revised and extended rear end, culminating in a sharply cut-off Kamm tail. In all, only 200 SZs were built, the minimum needed to homologate the car for production GT car racing, although the cleverness of the design made it a thoroughly practical proposition as a genuine long-distance roadgoing GT car as well as a thoroughbred track machine.

If the Giulietta SZ represented brute performance, the Bertone Giulietta

the performance to rival altogether much more expensive creations. With the same high-performance version of the Giulietta engine and the same five-speed gearbox as the SZ, Bertone's coupé had the same top speed, but its more comfortable interior won it a wider public. As it was also cheaper than the Zagato version, it also sold in greater numbers. In all, 1,366 were made in five years of production, but it would remain a rarity in Britain: when *Autosport* tested a privately owned Giulietta SS in early 1960, it

Continued overleaf

The Giulietta SZ and SS ... and Giulia SS

Continued from previous page

claimed that it was the only one in the country.

Subsequently the Bertone-bodied Giulietta SS took on the new 1600cc engine and became the Giulia SS, appearing for the first time in this guise at the Geneva Show in March 1963. This time it was fitted with the same higher-performance version of

the engine that was fitted to the Spider Veloce, and with its more efficient aerodynamics this took the top speed past the 125mph (200kph) mark. It cost 13 per cent more than the Sprint GT, itself one of the more expensive cars in the range, so it was never going to sell in large numbers. For all that, it just outdid its Giulietta SS predecessor, with 1,400 being made in two years of production.

RIGHT:
Was the Sprint Speciale the most beautiful Alfa of all time? Fashions change, but Bertone's design seems to have taken on the mantle of an all-time classic. (LAT)

There was less of an austere competition style to the interior of the Sprint Speciale. (LAT)

Last of the line: the 1300 Sprint of 1963–65. (Alfa Romeo archives)

Buying Hints

1. Both the Spider and the Sprint are hand-built cars of all-welded construction, so panels cannot simply be unbolted and replaced with better second-hand items. Standards of construction are high, but protection against rust non-existent.

2. Restoration-project UK-sourced Spiders tend to be basket cases, owing to old age and the British climate. Cars are not only much more plentiful in the States, but almost certain to be in better condition.

3. The sills on a Spider are a complex 11-section structure and can flatter to deceive: new or carefully filled outer sills can hide a corroded diaphragm and inner sill, while the generally corrosion-free curved inner sill can lull you into a false sense of security. As with all open cars, the evenness or otherwise of the door gaps is a good guide both to structural rigidity and to the quality of any repairs carried out. Gaps should be even top-to-bottom and side-to-side: be suspicious in particular of any car where the gap is tight at the top of the door and wide at the bottom, or vice-versa. This suggests either that the car is folding in the middle or that it has been incorrectly supported during work on the sills. If the doors do not shut properly your alarm bells should ring – and do not be fobbed off by a line about the catches needing adjusting . . .

4. Still on Spiders, lift the carpet in the rear luggage and spare-wheel well and check for rust at the join of the floorpan and the rear wheelarch; the latter area is also vulnerable on the Sprint.

5. Other Spider rust spots are the footwells and the rear floors; also – in common with the Sprint – the thinly double-skinned wheelarches and the bottom of the front and rear wings, as well as around the headlamps. Test for filler with a magnet – it will drop off if there is filler in the panel.

6. On both Spider and Sprint the rearmost corners of the boot can rot through, especially on the right-hand side, where the battery is located; the boot may also hole at the junction with the rear of the wheelarches.

7. Double-skinning of the boot and bonnet lids means that on both models corrosion can set in around the perimeter of the inner skins.

8. A shield on Sprints is intended to keep road dirt away from the scuttle and A-posts. In fact, dirt penetrates the shield, causing corrosion at the bottom of the front wings in line with this supposedly protective panel.

9. The front panels of the Sprint/Spider are vulnerable to accident damage: do not be surprised to find dents or filler here.

10. Replacement original bumpers are near-impossible to locate, and command high prices for even barely acceptable blades suitable for re-chroming. Repro bumpers are available for the Spider but their quality is disappointing. Be wary, therefore, of 'racerised' cars without bumpers. Be warned, too, that the rear bumpers tend to accumulate road dirt and rot out from behind. The mazak door handles are prone to pitting but may be reclaimable by a top-rank plater; replacements are available – at a price.

11. The Sprint is trimmed in a cloth/vinyl combination. The correct material is available from an American firm specialising in trim materials for classic Alfas so there is no need to lose sleep over a tatty but complete interior.

12. Veloce versions with their dual twin-choke Weber carbs are often poorly tuned, causing drivability problems; town use could have also caused plug fouling.

13. All the Giulietta Sprint Speciales, together with the first 170 Giulietta SZs, the first 200 Giulia Sprint Speciales, the first 7,000 Giulia Sprints and the first 5,600 Giulia Spiders, had front drum brakes with three leading shoes. Beautifully engineered, these brakes are not cheap to refurbish.

14. Whatever the body style of Giulia, the later the model the more evolved its mechanicals: faced with a choice between a 750 series car and a 101 series car, and with all other things being equal, it would be logical to go for the 101. But all other things are not equal: the longer-wheelbase 101 series Spider is considered by Alfa enthusiasts to have lost some of the immediacy of its predecessor, and so commands lower prices.

2000 & 2600
Saloons, Coupés & Spiders

For most buyers, Alfa Romeo's first post-war generations were predominantly made up of the 1900s, Giuliettas and Giulias. But for those who wanted something a little larger, more luxurious and undeniably more expensive, the company continued to manufacture a range with bigger engines, bigger bodies, bigger price-tags, and smaller numbers in terms of total production.

This began in 1958, with the introduction of a new design based on the final production version of the 1900 engine. This had been increased to 1975cc for the 1900 Super, and the

version used for the new Alfa Romeo 2000 was an uprated unit with an 8.25:1 compression ratio and a single double-choke carburettor, delivering 105bhp. This was fitted into a large, square-cut six-seater saloon body with a longer wheelbase and wider track than the 1900, but with the same suspension arrangements as the rest of the company's range.

The 2000 was 4cwt (200kg) heavier than the 1900. Nevertheless, with a five-speed gearbox, albeit controlled by a cumbersome steering-column change, it was capable of a genuine 100mph (160kph) top speed. The

The 2000 Berlina's square-cut lines were typical of its time, and had less of a distinguishably Alfa feel than the company's other models. (Alfa Romeo archives)

undistinguished styling did at least include a generous window area, and the company's claimed objective for the car was a combination of easy and comfortable high-speed touring for up to six people. However, its price was 60 per cent up on the Giulietta TI of almost equivalent performance, which limited its appeal to all but those who needed to move large groups of people, and in consequence relatively few were sold. In three years of production, the total only amounted to 2,799.

However, another variant that appeared at the same time did rather better. This was the Pininfarina-bodied 2000 Spider, which had a shorter chassis with the same front and rear track, and a rather more powerful version of the engine with

The idea was to provide comfortable high-speed touring for up to six people

an 8.5:1 compression ratio and a pair of double-choke carburettors to boost power to 115bhp. This also had the five-speed gearbox, but controlled by a much more effective floor-mounted lever, and the spacious two-seater body provided two additional occasional seats at the back.

Unlike the saloon, the 2000 Spider had a much closer family resemblance to its smaller-engined stablemates in the company range, although most people felt that the stretched design, which was actually by Touring rather than Pininfarina, was less effective than it was in the 1300 and 1600 versions. It was appreciably lighter than the saloon, at a total weight of 23.2cwt (1,180kg), but its top speed of 109mph (175kph) was slightly disappointing for such a large and imposing car.

2000 Berlina
1958–1961

ENGINE:
Four-cylinder, twin ohc
Bore x stroke | 84.5 x 88mm
Capacity | 1975cc
Power | 105bhp

TRANSMISSION:
Four-speed gearbox
Final drive: | 4.777:1

BODY STYLE:
Four-door saloon

PERFORMANCE:
(from contemporary sources)
Max speed | 100mph (160kph)

LENGTH: | 15ft 8in (4.78m)

WIDTH: | 5ft 5.4in (1.66m)

WHEELBASE: | 8ft 9in (2.72m)

2000 Spider
1958–61

As 2000 Berlina, except:
Power | 115bhp
Max speed | 109mph (175kph)
0–60mph (97kph) | 14.2 seconds

BODY STYLE: | 2+2-seater roadster

LENGTH: | 14ft 9in (4.50m)

WIDTH: | 5ft 5.4in (1.66m)

WHEELBASE: | 8ft 2.5in (2.50m)

2000 Sprint
1960–1962

As 2000 Spider, except:
BODY STYLE: | 2+2 coupé

LENGTH: | 14ft 10in (4.53m)

WHEELBASE: | 8ft 5.5in (2.58m)

2600 Berlina
1962–68

As 2000 Berlina, except:
ENGINE:
Six-cylinder, twin ohc
Bore x stroke | 83 x 79.6mm
Capacity | 2,584cc
Power | 130bhp

TRANSMISSION:
Four-speed gearbox
Final drive: | 5.125:1

PERFORMANCE:
(from contemporary sources)
Max speed | 109mph (175kph)

2600 Spider
1962–65

As 2600 Berlina, except:
Power | 145bhp
Max speed | 124mph (203kph)
0–60mph (97kph) | 11.1 seconds

BODY STYLE: | 2+2-seater roadster

LENGTH: | 14ft 9in (4.50m)

WIDTH: | 5ft 5.4in (1.66m)

WHEELBASE: | 8ft 1in (2.50m)

2600 Sprint
1962–66

As 2600 Spider, except:
BODY STYLE: | 2+2-seater coupé

LENGTH: | 14ft 10in (4.53m)

WHEELBASE: | 8ft 5.5in (2.58m)

NUMBER BUILT:
2000 Berlina	2,799
2000 Spider	3,443
2000 Sprint	700
2600 Berlina	2,092
2600 Spider	2,255
2600 Sprint	6,999
2600 Sprint Zagato	105

The 2000 Spider was a large, spacious and handsome sports car, but rather under-powered with just a 2-litre engine. (LAT)

When the Giulietta was replaced by the Giulia in 1962, a similar shake-up happened in this bigger-car section of the company's range. This was no mere substitution of another version of the existing engine with slightly different dimensions. It was something much more radical – a return to a six-cylinder engine for production Alfas for the first time since pre-war days. On the other hand, it was not a new design, but a clever reworking of the classic 'four'.

What Alfa's engineers did was to reduce the bore very slightly, from 84.5mm to 83mm, and reduce the stroke much more radically, from 88mm to 79.6mm. This gave the engine 'oversquare' proportions in accordance with current thinking. They then added a pair of extra cylinders to give a capacity of 2584cc. Unlike the original 1975cc engine, which had been built with a cast-iron block like its 1900 predecessor, the new unit was cast in

than that of the saloon. What buyers got for their money was a large, handsome coupé with room for four people in reasonable comfort, but in two years of production only 700 were made.

The businesslike layout of the Spider dashboard. (LAT)

The Spider was barely more expensive than the 2000 saloon, and did at least have a whiff of sporting appeal about it, in spite of its size. This enabled it to do rather better in total output, with 3,443 being snapped up by eager buyers in three years of production. By then the third of the 2000 range had made its appearance.

This was the 2000 Sprint, which was a longer and wider antecedent to Bertone's later and better-known Giulia Sprint. The larger dimensions suited the proportions well, and its elegant lines were graced by a larger version of the traditional Alfa Romeo shield-shaped grille on the front, flanked by dual headlamps. It shared the engine of the 2000 Spider, giving it similar acceleration and top speed, and it was the most expensive of the three, with a price 20 per cent more

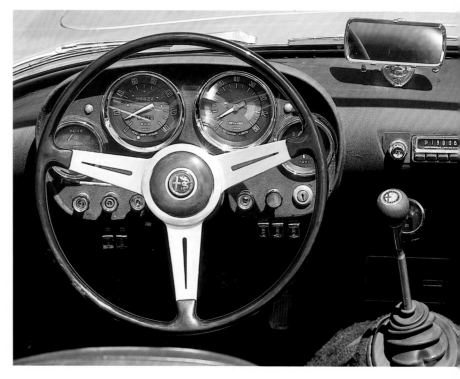

valves inclined at right angles to one another (compared to the 80 degrees of the smaller engines), each one actuated by a chain-driven overhead camshaft.

The new 2600 saloon used a 130bhp version of the engine, with an 8.5:1 compression ratio and a lone double-choke carburettor. After the first year of production, the original combination of disc brakes at the front and drums at the rear was changed to servo-assisted discs all round, and although the weight was increased by 90lb (40kg), the extra power was enough to lift the top speed to 109mph (175kph). This was appreciably better than its predecessor, and equivalent to the performance of the 2000 Sprint and Spider. Surprisingly, to keep the six-seat capacity of the car, the company retained the front bench seat until the 1965 model-year and never deviated from a steering-column gearchange, which rather diluted the appeal of the splendid Alfa gearbox.

The new Spider and Sprint took another step up the power scale, with

The 2600 saloon had different front and rear treatments from the 2000, and hid beneath the bonnet a larger, smoother and more powerful six-cylinder version of the classic Alfa Romeo twin-cam engine. (Alfa Romeo archives)

light alloy, as were the Giulietta and Giulia engines. In all other respects, the engine's ancestry showed through clearly, with hemispherical combustion chambers, a single row of plugs in the centre of each combustion space, and two rows of

The big six-cylinder twin-cam engine that powered the 2600 range was a surprisingly easy fit, even under the bonnet of the Spider. (LAT)

The 2600 Spider differed from the 2000 in having quarterlights and a changed treatment for the side grilles. (Alfa Romeo archives)

lower portion of the side panelling was replaced by a single strip. The 2600 Sprint was the least changed, with just an air scoop on the bonnet and chrome '2600' badging replacing the original '2000' on the sides and boot, but it remained a potent reminder of the kind of cars that Alfa had turned out before the war, where speed, character and comfort had been combined in designs that earned the company a place of honour in the automotive history books.

The Spider had a similar specification and a similar performance to the Sprint. Both models began their production run with disc brakes at the front and drums at the back, although before long they were changed to the same servo-assisted all-disc layout as the saloon. Both models were considerably more spacious than the smaller Alfas, and while they lacked their sporting character they had a refined personality of their own.

The saloon remained in production for six years, from late 1962. In all that time, a grand total of 2,092 was made, including 54 of the 2600 Berlina De Luxe version. This was an attractive reworking of the body style by OSI, with a much fresher and more fashionable streamlined shape that suited the car's ample proportions very well. The Sprint and Spider only remained in production for half that time. During those three years 6,999 Sprints were made, and another 2,255 Spiders. Total production of the 2600 series added up to 11,346 in all, more than half as much again as the number of 2000s.

Hidden within those figures was a much more significant total for UK

a version of the six-cylinder engine fitted with three double-choke carburettors, a 9:1 compression ratio and a power output of 145bhp at 5,900rpm. This was enough, thanks to a weight reduction over the saloon of 1.2cwt (60kg), to provide a top speed of 125mph (200kph) and much more exhilarating performance. There were some detailed styling changes. For example, the bonnet line of the Berlina was raised and flattened, and a pair of extra headlamps fitted inboard of the originals. The Spider now had swivelling quarter lights, and the double chrome strip along the

RIGHT:
The 2600 Sprint was in effect a larger version of the Bertone style later found on the Sprint series of the coupés. (Alfa Romeo archives)

The Bertone 2600 Sprint badge. (LAT)

buyers. Fully 103 of the Spiders were made in right-hand-drive form, most of them for the British market. There were also 597 right-hand-drive Sprints and, rather more surprisingly, no fewer than 425 of the saloons. Clearly British customers were being wooed with a choice of models that now extended right across the company's range, even though the larger Alfas represented but a small fraction of the firm's total production.

Finding either of these big Alfas in their saloon guise is not going to be easy. In any case, Alfa fanciers are more likely to be in pursuit of a Spider or Sprint – and more likely to find one. Will such people be disappointed? If they expect the delicacy of a Giulietta, the answer is 'yes'. If, on the other hand, they appreciate high-grade engineering, whether or not it has an overtly sporting character, then they will find that the cars have a real – if somewhat oddball – appeal.

The 2000 engine has to propel a fairly weighty motor car, and performance, while refined – turbine-like, even – is relatively soft-edged. The same can be said of the chassis, not helped by steering that is on the low-geared side: there is a relaxed aura to the progress of a 2000 Spider or Sprint

that is some way removed from the firm and instant nature of a Giulietta's or Giulia's responses.

Turn to the 2600 and you have more weight up front, giving a not unexpected dose of pronounced understeer and body roll, plus steering that seems even slower-witted. At four turns lock-to-lock, the latter is no illusion, but at least the steering box has the lack of slop traditional to all Alfas. The slick spring-loaded gearchange is again typical Alfa, and the all-disc brakes of sporting 2600s are admirably effective without demanding excessive effort.

As for the engine, triple-Solexed in Spider/Sprint form, it lugs as only a straight-six can, but if you ask it to rev it does so with a crisp responsiveness in line with its sporting twin-cam credentials; even in the less highly tuned saloon format the performance of the 2582cc 'six' gives no cause for complaint – 130bhp (net) was after all a pretty impressive figure for the time, even if

The cockpit of this immaculate 2600 Sprint also features a radio and a Halda Speedpilot for classic car rallying. (LAT)

15bhp down on the output of the Sprint/Spider engine.

In the end, the big Alfa 'sixes' never really did as well as the company hoped or expected. The underlying objective, to give Alfa Romeo a stake in the bigger-car class to match its closest rivals, was too expensive a proposition for the development and production costs involved. A much better and more economical alternative was to modify the smaller cars by fitting a larger engine and introducing a more luxurious specification. The Giulia was due to

The OSI-bodied version of the 2600 Berlina – in all, 54 were built. (Alfa Romeo archives)

be supplemented by the bigger and more powerful 1750 range as 1967 gave way to 1968, and this was the signal for the dropping of the six-cylinder cars. The Spider had already been phased out in 1965, with the Sprint following a year later. The Berlina lasted till 1968, but by then the future belonged to the four-cylinder Alfas once again.

Zagato made 105 of these 2600 SZ coupés between 1964 and 1966. (LAT)

Buying Hints

1. You have to be dedicated to search out one of these cars: the saloons are near-extinct in the UK, and examples of the Sprint coupé and the Touring-bodied Spider are few and far between.

2. The remarks on the 1900 engine apply equally to the development of the unit used in the 2000; as for the 2600 engine, this is more prone to head-gasket problems than the 2000, but otherwise has no particular weaknesses. As a 'six', rebuilding the 2600 engine is a more expensive operation than is the case with a regulation 'four': a set of pistons and liners will cost more than twice as much as a set for a Giulia.

3. The bodies are strong but vulnerable to rust in the wheelarches (especially the front arches, which are double-skinned), the front valance, the sills, and – eventually – the floors.

4. Triple Solex twin-choke carburettors are used on the 2600 Sprint, Spider and Zagato; these are not easy to adjust correctly, so poor drivability is common. Some cars have been converted to triple Webers, with the beneficial side-effect of increased performance.

The Duetto &
1750 & 2000 *Spiders*

The original (and many say the best) Duetto, with Dustin Hoffman look-alike, celebrating the car's starring role in the classic 1966 film *The Graduate*. This is the round-tailed 1.6-litre version. Initially buyers were restricted in their choice of colours to red or white, but later the choice was widened; however, the car always looked particularly attractive in the traditional Alfa Romeo red. (LAT)

Following the success of the Giulia TI and the Sprint GT, there was one survivor from the Giulietta range that was overdue for replacement. The Spider had continued in production until 1965, unchanged apart from the larger engine, greater power, a change of name and a switch to disc brakes on the front wheels.

In 1966, with the introduction of the Veloce version of the Sprint GT, it was time for the appearance of the new Spider. This was to be the last design created by Battista Pininfarina himself. In its basic treatment, the new car dated back to a show car design of 1962, which had a similarly scalloped treatment to the side panelling, and which was actually a Pininfarina version of the Giulietta Sprint Speciale. Some commentators also claimed to see similarities with the experimental *Disco Volante* (Flying Saucer) racing prototypes of the early 1950s, although that resemblance was even more distant.

The new 1600 Spider was a much more radical redesign than was apparent to the casual viewer. It was based on the Giulia 105 series chassis,

The cockpit of the Duetto, with the two main dials on the plastic-covered binnacle behind the steering wheel, the subsidiary dials angled towards the driver, a painted metal dash and rubber floor covering. (LAT)

rather than the Giulietta chassis of the previous Spider, which in this form – shared with the GTV, GTA and Giulia Super – owed many of its components, including the heavy-duty wider-track front suspension and the all-round disc brakes, to the redoubtable Tubolare. The wheelbase was unchanged from the previous Spider, but because the new design had longer front and rear overhangs, the car was about a foot longer than its predecessor and better streamlined.

A controversial feature of the styling was the car's long and rounded tail, which it shared with the 1962 Pininfarina show car. The Italians called it 'the Cuttlefish', and looking at the contours of the body it is easy to see why. Yet the shape is clean and well balanced, and with the advantage of hindsight what began as uncomfortably new and

unconventional now seems an exercise in classic simplicity. Where one member of the *Road and Track* test team said, on first seeing the car in 1966, that it was a 'contrived design with meaningless styling gimmicks', 21 years later *Thoroughbred & Classic Car* could say of the same design that its shape 'is pure and simple, with an elegance that few other sports cars can match'.

Some features did not wear well with time, such as the plastic headlamp covers, which were outlawed on the US market, and which almost certainly reduced the intensity of the headlamp beams. Inside the car's design showed a comforting order of priorities. The snug, wrap-around bucket seats were set low down in the cockpit, so driver and passenger had their legs stretched out in an almost horizontal position. Big circular dials for the speedometer and tachometer were set in the driver's line of sight on a small plastic-covered panel, with smaller instruments showing fuel tank contents, water temperature and oil pressure set in the centre of the painted-metal dash but angled towards the driver.

1600 Spider Duetto
1966–1967

ENGINE:
Four-cylinder, twin ohc

Bore x stroke	78 x 82mm
Capacity	1570cc
Power	92bhp
	(Veloce 112bhp)
Max speed	113mph (181kph)
0–60mph (97kph)	11.3 seconds

LENGTH: 13ft 11.3in (3.90m)

WIDTH: 5ft 4.2in (1.63m)

1750 Spider Veloce
Kamm tail

As 1600 Spider Duetto except:
ENGINE:

Capacity	1779cc
Power	122bhp

PERFORMANCE:
(from contemporary sources)

Max speed	118mph (190kph)
0–60mph (97kph)	9.2 seconds

LENGTH: 13ft 6in (4.12m)

2000 Spider
1991

As 1600 Spider Duetto except:
ENGINE:

Capacity	1962cc
Power	132bhp at 5500rpm

PERFORMANCE:
(both from *Autocar* – American test figures are slightly slower)

Max speed	119mph (192kph)
0–60mph (97kph)	9.8 seconds

NUMBER BUILT:

1300 Spider Junior	7,237
1600 Spider	13,465
1600 Spider Duetto	6,325
1750 Spider	8,722
2000 Spider	88,240

The neat gear lever, as with all the Alfa five-speed changes, was spring-biased towards the central third–fourth plane to simplify speedy shifting, once the knack of letting the lever find its own way home was mastered. The old spartan finish of earlier Alfas, apparent in the absence of wood and abundance of painted metal, was echoed in the rubber floormats, although these were embossed with the Alfa badge as an additional gesture to the car's pedigree. There was room behind the seats for luggage, although a token amount of upholstery allowed the possibility of accommodating a pair of small children in those pre-seatbelt days. Meanwhile, thanks to the longer tail, the boot space, although shallow, was larger than in the earlier Spider.

Under the dash was a pair of matched levers for choke and hand throttle. Thanks to accelerator pumps on the two double-choke Webers, the choke was almost superfluous, since a couple of tramps on the throttle pedal enabled first-time starting even on the coldest days. Steering column levers controlled lights and indicators, and as with earlier Alfas what appeared to be a floor-mounted dipswitch actually squirted the screen with washer fluid and applied a couple of strokes of the wipers when instant visibility was needed.

The hood was simplicity itself. Raising it involved grabbing a central handle on the front rim and pulling it up to the windscreen rail, then snapping two chromed over-centre clips into

The first changes to the body design were at the back, where the rounded tail was given the chopped-off Kamm treatment; seen here on a 1977 2000 Spider, 1750 Spiders were first given this treatment. (LAT)

By the time the 2000 Spider had been introduced, other detail changes had been made, including recessed door-handles. (LAT)

the corners at the rear of the wind-up windows in the doors, but that could be left for later without the whole thing catching the wind.

When the weather improved, lowering the hood was equally simple, compared with some sports cars where the hood had to be removed completely and the frame folded and carefully stowed in the boot. Uncovering the Spider meant snapping those chrome clips free, raising the hood from the screen rail and pushing it back towards the rear of the car, when the whole thing collapsed back into pre-set folds. Once again, if time allowed the whole thing could be tidied up, and the car came with a hood cover that finished the job in a shipshape fashion.

position. With practice, and a little agility, it was possible to do it without leaving the driving seat, if it started to rain when the car was stuck in a traffic jam. To finish the job, a pair of Velcro strips anchored the hood to

The front end was also changed, because of stricter safety regulations, as shown in this graphic head-to-head comparison. (LAT)

Naming the Spider – Stalin or Hitler?

At its launch just about the only thing the new Spider 1600 lacked was a name. Its official designation was indistinguishable from that of its predecessor, which was a strange way for the company to celebrate such a new and successful design. With the Alfa Romeo 1600 Spider, the Alfa Romeo 1600 Giulia Spider and the Alfa Romeo 1600 Spider Veloce having between them two different chassis, two different body styles and a host of different parts, there was bound to be confusion among customers, owners, dealers, mechanics and suppliers of spares, and the only way to regularise the situation was to give the new car an identity of its own.

Within a few months of its introduction Alfa announced a competition to suggest a name, offering one of the cars to the winner. The response was enormous: 140,000 suggestions poured into the factory during the eight week competition period, the majority from Italy, but overseas entries from countries as far afield as

South Africa and the Far East accounted for more than 10 per cent of the total.

The variety of the suggestions was staggering. Some were based on conventional images of speed and power: Panther, Wolf and Leopard (or their Italian equivalents). Others took note of the shape of the car – Sole and Piranha – while others followed the Giulietta-Giulia theme with Patricia and Lucia. But these were pedestrian and respectable compared with some of the more off-the-wall proposals: the geographical (Acapulco, Costa Smeralda), the celebrity-conscious (Nuvolari, Lollobrigida, Zatopek, Brigitte Bardot), the monosyllabic (Gin, Surf, Strip, Goal), the cultural (Michelangelo, Shakespeare) and the frankly bizarre (Pizza, Edelweiss, Al Capone, Stalin and Hitler). In the end, the company played safe, and one Guidobaldi Trionfi from Brescia turned up at the factory to be presented with the keys for a brand-new car, for suggesting the name 'Duetto'.

One question on which almost all the testers agreed from the very beginning was that the new Spider was very much a case of handsome is as handsome does. *Road and Track* qualified its initially unkind remarks about the car's styling, in the same test. 'If no one on the staff was wild about [its] appearance, exactly the opposite was true about driving the car,' it wrote. 'Everybody loved it. The overall impression is one of great responsiveness, and the feeling that the car is an extension of the driver at the controls is unmistakably clear.'

If the Spider had a limitation in the roadholding department, it was a problem it had in common with its

predecessor. As the Giulietta Spider gave way to the Giulia, the larger engine increased a tendency towards nose-heaviness, 54 per cent of the car's weight being over the front wheels. In the case of the 1600 Spider, the effect of the longer front overhang increased the figure to 56 per cent. In practice, the only way this tended to manifest itself was a certain lack of traction in soft or icy conditions, but it never seemed to make any difference in ordinary handling.

The only other problem was, once again, a drawback that the car inherited from the earlier models. This was a certain lack of accommodation for taller drivers. Many Italian cars have apparently

Publicity for the Duetto was helped by its role in two films of the time

been designed for the stature of the typical Italian driver, and more importantly in the ratio between length of arm and length of leg. The drawback for the tallest drivers was not only that the top of the head would press against the hood when it was in place, but the windscreen top cut into the field of view. In addition, a seat position with the pedals at a comfortable distance very often put the steering wheel too far away for comfort. *Road and Track* speculated bitterly that this might be due to Alfa's chief styling engineer being able to touch his toes without bending over, but there was a deal of truth in the criticism.

Nevertheless, the car was an improvement in several ways. Other plus points identified by testers included a lack of the body roll, which was still noticeable in its Giulietta and Giulia stablemates. With the same engine, carburation and state of tune as the GTV, the car was capable of a top speed of 113mph (180kph), with brisk acceleration. *Motor* summed up the car's attractions succinctly in its initial road-test when it said that 'the performance is good, the roadholding excellent, and the handling superb'. Seen against this kind of praise, the fact that the car was actually comparable in price in Britain to the E-type Jaguar and the Lotus Elan became slightly less important. But it still meant that it needed all the praise it was capable of earning.

Fortunately, in sales terms, the car did very well. In just over a year 6,325 were sold, representing an encouraging increase over the best production figures for its predecessor. By the time a name had been chosen to differentiate it more clearly from its forebears, the Duetto, as it was now tagged, became more widely accepted in its own right, and Alfa Romeo went to great lengths to market the car as widely as possible. Three of the cars were sent across the Atlantic in May 1966 on the liner *Rafaello* to be put on show in New York, and publicity was helped by its starring role in two films of the time. Future James Bond star Roger Moore drove a right-hand-drive car in the movie *Crossplot*, but a much more memorable appearance was made by a red left-hand-drive Spider in *The Graduate* as the personal transport of the hero Ben Braddock, played by Dustin Hoffman.

Autodelta set to work on a competition version of the car, intended for Group 3 Touring Car races; it delivered 160bhp at 7,500 rpm, and had a top speed of 134mph (215kph). This variant was shown at the Turin Sports Car Show in February 1968, but already the car on which it was based was bowing out in favour of a revamped and more powerful version. And with it went the name that Alfa Romeo had gone to such lengths to give it.

For the introduction of the 1750 range, the Giulia engine was bored and stroked from 1570cc to 1779cc. With the kind of poetic licence common in marketing departments, this allowed Alfa to recall the glories of the past by borrowing the 1750 designation used for the immortal two-seaters of the late 1920s and early '30s. This time the company managed to synchronise the launch properly so that all three cars – the Berlina, the Sprint GT coupé and the Spider – appeared side by side.

There were sound reasons for not perpetuating the Duetto name. Two of the most pressing were that this was a member of a prestigious new range that Alfa wanted to emphasise, not a hangover from the previous group of models, and any repeat of the previous confusion over the car and its predecessor was definitely to be avoided. Second, the whole point of choosing the 1750 name for the new models was to create a link with the two-seater open roadsters of the past, and the Spider was the most obvious descendant in this respect. So the 1750 Spider it had to be, from the very beginning this time. It was

An increasing tendency towards middle-aged spread was blurring the lines of the original concept, with heavier bumpers and an air dam on the rear bootlid, although the excellent hood was still easy to raise and lower. (LAT)

The inside of the car was becoming more and more lavishly padded. (LAT)

actually referred to by Alfa as the 1750 Spider Veloce, although there was no standard Spider to necessitate the Veloce distinction.

There were other changes too. The braking system was given servo assistance and an alternator replaced the dynamo. The engine was given a stiffer cylinder block, and the wheels were widened in section and reduced in diameter, with the 155-15s used for the Giulietta and Giulia ranges being replaced by 165-14s. Finally, the front suspension geometry was modified, to raise the roll centre and allow the use of marginally softer springing. In addition, the transverse link in the traditional rigid axle rear suspension was revised, to reduce production costs, and a rear anti-roll bar was fitted.

The 1750s first made their appearance at the Brussels Motor Show early in 1968. But the prospects

for sales in the USA ran into problems, as US requirements on emission control were already advancing ahead of those in the Old World. This imposed a heavy additional burden on a specialist maker such as Alfa Romeo. Not only did it have to develop a special version purely for the American market, but it also had to produce a third version to meet Californian requirements, which differed again from those of other states.

The biggest difference with the American version was a switch from the traditional pair of double-choke Weber carburettors to mechanical fuel injection. This used a metering pump made by Spica, an Alfa subsidiary, and which was originally designed for lorry engines. The mechanism was redesigned to match the requirements of the 1750 engine, and incorporated a toothed belt connected to the engine crankshaft, which drove the pump at half engine speed. Inside, the pump worked like an engine in reverse, with a miniature crankshaft actuating four variable-displacement plungers, one for each cylinder, through a set of small connecting rods.

Fuel was supplied through a normal electric pump, and the displacement of the plungers was dictated by the throttle opening at any moment, thereby controlling the amount of fuel injected into each individual cylinder, and the precise time in the engine cycle. Other parts of the system were able to take into account the effects of cold weather and engine temperature.

Other differences between the American version of the 1750 Spider and the European versions included an ugly additional bumper bar across the front of the elegant little Alfa radiator shield. The American version's differential also retained the old Duetto final drive ratio of 4.56:1 instead of the 4.10:1 unit of the European 1750s.

Although the engine was appreciably bigger, the performance was only slightly improved over that of the Duetto. The larger unit delivered 122bhp at 5,500rpm, but the real difference was provided by a 30 per cent increase in the peak torque, which improved the flexibility and responses of the car. Top speed was only slightly increased, to 118mph (190kph), but the car now reached 60mph from a standing start in 9.2 seconds instead of 11.2 seconds. In

For most of its production life the Spider in all its different models was available with a series of substantial but expensive hardtops, although these are a very rare sight on surviving vehicles – this was a 1986 option. (Alfa Romeo archives)

all body details, the car was virtually indistinguishable from the Duetto.

Nevertheless, there were differences in handling, with the smaller, wider wheels. Testers reported that the rear anti-roll bar was too stiff, and caused the inside rear wheel to lift under hard cornering loads, causing a degree of wheelspin under power. Contrastingly, others insisted that the result was a reduction in the 'traditional Alfa understeer'. Certainly the ride seemed to have improved over rough surfaces, and the car's structure showed no tendency towards flexing or scuttle shake.

Once again, those customers who wanted the looks and the performance at lower cost were catered for by a backwards nod in the direction of the Giulietta. When the 1750 Spider Veloce moved in to replace the Duetto, Alfa also introduced a cheaper 1290cc Giulietta-engined version with a 9:1 compression ratio and twin double-choke Webers, this combination delivering 103bhp and a top speed of more than 106mph (170kph). For a car that sold at just over three-quarters the price of the 1750, this was a real bargain, and 7,237 Spider 1300s were made in ten years of production. Manufacture ended in 1978, by which time those seeking a cheaper Spider were more satisfactorily catered for by a 1600cc Spider Junior. This had been introduced in 1972, and continued through to 1992.

Meanwhile, the 1750 Spider almost doubled this output in just three years. In 1970 the body was extensively revamped. The 'cuttlefish' shape vanished into the history books and the car now ended in a more sharply cut-off Kamm tail,

The inside of the car was becoming progressively more luxurious and rather less sporty, in common with the Berlinas and Sprint GTVs.

which was claimed to increase the boot space. Oddly, *Road and Track* complained that it actually reduced the *useable* boot space by nearly 10 per cent! Other changes included moving the indicator repeater lights forward of the front wheels instead of behind them, and fitting new recessed door handles.

Inside, the finish was more luxurious, with headrests, a deeply dished steering wheel, cowls for the main instruments in front of the driver, and a console between the footwells to carry rocker switches and heater controls. Instead of a short gear lever projecting directly from the floor, it now protruded through an opening in the console, and some said that this made the shift action rather awkward.

By 1971 a total of 6,769 Spider Veloces had been made. Nearly half of these had been sold in the USA, although development delays with the complex but eventually efficient fuel-injection system had taken the car off the American market in 1968 and again in 1970; over that period a mere 633 of the carburettored cars had been made with right-hand-drive. But bigger and better things were in prospect, and in June 1971 Alfa announced the new 2000 Spider Veloce.

This stretched the 1900/Giulietta/Giulia/1750 engine yet again. By enlarging the bores from 80mm to 84mm, the engine capacity was increased to 1962cc, giving dimensions remarkably close to those of the 1900 Super and 2000 engines. In bodywork and appointments the 2000 Spider was the same as the 1970 version of the 1750 Spider Veloce, and its mechanical specification was also similar, with a 9:1 compression ratio and two double-choke Webers, with fuel-injection reserved for the American market.

However, the increase in capacity boosted the power to 133bhp at 5,500rpm, with torque to match.

Oddly, the published tests showed little improvement in top speed or standing-start acceleration, although there were undoubted improvements in flexibility and mid-range response. Although not everyone agreed that the styling improved on that of the original Duetto, there was little doubt that this version of the Spider had a pleasing combination of character and performance. All of which was important, as this final version would remain in production long after the rest of the range had been replaced.

Later Spiders not only looked heavier and less sporty, but the character and feel of the car seemed to age with the change in its lines. The switch to the

By 1971 some 6,769 Spider Veloces had been made – almost half sold in the USA

2000 engine added a lot of useful low-speed torque, but owners complained of a harshness at higher revs that contrasted with the ever-willing qualities of the original 1570cc unit. The 2000 also had a limited-slip differential and from 1975 a pair of massive energy-absorbing bumpers, which obscured the neatly styled front-end and radiator shield of the original. In 1983 these were revised to include a black plastic Alfa grille, together with a soft spoiler on the cut-off tail. By then the car's interior had been given the luxury treatment with options including electric windows, electrically operated mirrors and, from 1982, air-conditioning. Mechanical modifications included variable valve timing from 1980, and a new intake manifold that made the starter and the fuel-injection pump almost completely inaccessible.

By now you have probably got the message about front-gearbox Alfas: the smaller-engined cars are sweeter, the bigger-engined cars more flexible

Spiders live on – and return to the UK

The 2000 Spider Veloce's saloon and coupé stablemates were taken out of production in 1977. This was also the original intention with the Spider, but when plans for a possible Alfetta Spider never proceeded beyond a concept car at the Turin Show, the original Spider had to remain in production for year after year, simply to meet the demands of customers who still believed that the best real Alfas had two seats and an open top. For UK customers, however, the future seemed bleak, since stricter Type Approval regulations introduced in 1978 persuaded Alfa that it was not worth making the expensive alterations to the design needed to meet them, and accordingly the right-hand-drive version was dropped.

Only in the early 1980s was the supply of Spiders for UK customers revived, and then only thanks to the Surrey-based Alfa Romeo dealer Bell & Colvill, who started to import Spiders from the Low Countries and carry out their own right-hand-drive conversion, rather as importers had done with the 1900s and Giuliettas decades before. By then the lovely original shape had been all but buried under thick rubber bumpers and a rear spoiler, but the bones were still there under the skin. The mechanical specification was almost unchanged, except that the two double-choke carburettors were now Dellortos rather than Webers.

So the Spider continued to appear on British roads well into the 1980s, and eventually the parent company realised the size of the opportunity that it was missing. Finally, in 1991 Alfa re-introduced the right-hand-drive Spider for British customers; its body, redesigned in 1990, now had reshaped boot and rear wings, colour-coded plastic front and rear bumpers, new sills and detailed cockpit changes. Even for the UK market the carburettors had been replaced by fuel injection, and the traditional engine was now fitted with automatically variable valve timing. In 1991 the car sold for £18,550, which was almost exactly ten times the price of the first Duetto, and it continued to be made until 1994.

The last Spiders, recognisable by their body-colour plastic bumpers, were soggier in their responses. (LAT)

The final 1990-onwards version of the tail was a neater treatment than the earlier Kamm, and was held by some to be better than the more complex design of the original Duetto. (LAT)

This was the final dashboard and trim fitted to the Spider, and seems a world away from the traditional layout of the Duetto. (LAT)

and muscular in their performance, and all are blessed with high levels of handling and roadholding, backed up by a deliciously fast and accurate gearchange. This is all as true of the Spiders as of the GTV coupés.

Early Spiders are pin-sharp in their responses, with a clarity of behaviour in line with their unadorned cockpit. Rewarding handling, a supple ride, and the delights of Alfa's twin-cam engine add up to an inviting combination of virtues. Dial in an excellent hood – erecting it really is a one-hand job – and strong brakes and it is not hard to see the appeal of these cars.

However, the long production run had its sad consequences: late cars seem soft and sloppy in comparison, and even seem more prone to scuttle

shake. What was ahead of the pack in the late 1960s really did seem off the pace by the standards of the '90s. Better, then, to go for a Spider from the classic era: the best money is on the sweet and competent square-tail 2000 from an era when the body was unsullied by US-market addenda and the engine breathed through a brace of Webers.

Buying Hints

1. Not surprisingly, the Duetto and Spider suffer from being open cars. A particularly charming eccentricity is that Alfa decided to run the drain hoses from the hood tray directly into the sills. As soon as the sill drain-slots clog, the sills fill with water . . . with the inevitable consequences. Check carefully, therefore, for rotten sills, and – even on supposedly well-restored cars – for poorly-executed repairs: the usual inspection of door fit will be a good guide to the car's soundness.

2. The rear of the front wings is vulnerable to rust, not least as the protective shield tends to act as a perfect trap for road dirt: corrosion along the line of this shield is not uncommon.

3. Front floors rust through from the inside, if water has lain in the footwells, and the rear floor is also vulnerable. The seat mountings, in the form of sealed box sections, can rot out if moisture has penetrated them. The spare-wheel well in the boot is also rust-prone, as a result of blockage of the well's drain-hole.

4. Late Spiders are particularly prone to rust around the front crossmember mountings in the inner wing area. As with other 105 series cars, the crossmember under the radiator is liable to rot through.

5. The round-tail models are hard to find and the double-skinned tail is prone to rust. Expect disappointments in your quest if you are after one of these early cars.

6. The pointed prow is very vulnerable to accident damage, and most cars have had at least one 'nose job'. On ex-US cars this may merely mean a good going over with filler.

7. The hood is excellent but not cheap to replace; additionally the front rail can rust through.

8. Interior trim items are available from British and American specialists.

9. The dashboard top on later US-sourced cars is often cracked owing to the action of Californian sun; covers for left-hand-drive dashes are available in the States, but are a poor substitute for the original.

10. Potential mechanical ailments are as all 105 series cars; as with the 1750/2000 GTVs, the relatively soft rear springs can sag.

11. Beware 1969–82 US-sourced cars with Spica mechanical fuel injection. This can be troublesome if the art of adjusting it correctly has not been mastered, and parts are hard to locate; converting to carbs is not difficult, and if you lack the patience to sort the injection set-up this is a sensible way around the problems. The later Bosch electronic injection is efficient and reliable. Note that US-market 1750/2000 Berlinas and GTVs also used the Spica injection from 1969 onwards.

12. Many left-hand-drive cars have been converted to right-hand-drive. Those adapted by respected Alfa dealer Bell & Colvill and using a right-hand-drive steering box are well-executed, but be cautious of lesser conversions using a left-hand-drive steering box on a specially fabricated bracket. If faced with a left-hand-drive car, before contemplating a conversion consider that the costs are not likely to be recovered on sale; it is no big deal driving a left-hooker anyway, and an ex-States car is a cheap way into Spidering.

1750 & 2000 *Saloons*

The Alfa 1750 Berlina body was a clever reworking by Bertone of the Alfa in-house design for the Giulia TI, and managed to make the car look bigger and more imposing while at the same time smoothing out the sharp edges. (Alfa Romeo archives)

When Alfa Romeo began to consider a replacement for the Giulia range in the mid-1960s there were two over-riding priorities. The nature of competition meant that any successful replacement would have to offer more power and performance, and preferably also more interior room. Second, it would have to be capable of maintaining the wide customer appeal of the Giulia range in all its variants, since this had already established itself as the company's best-selling design of all time, outdoing even the successful and long-lived Giulietta. In 1961, the peak year for Giulietta production, 35,711 cars had left the factory, but this rate was more than doubled by its successor. In 1967, the peak year for Giulia production, 72,763 cars were made.

In that same year, the bigger six-cylinder Alfas were still being

produced. As a measure of comparison, only 56 of those were made during 1967, and in the following two years just 30 more would be made. Although this was a decline from the more successful years of the 'sixes', it was clear that the trouble and expense of updating these models would hardly be likely to pay off in commercial success. The other option was to upgrade the much more successful four-cylinder cars to deliver the extra performance needed to match competitors such as BMW, which Alfa's management had long regarded as its principal overseas rival.

The objective was logical enough, but the way in which Alfa set out to achieve it proved much more difficult to understand. Where BMW had taken its well-proven 2-litre engine and fitted it into the compact 1600 model to produce instant performance without any of the usual development costs and delays, Alfa had no existing larger engine to do the job for them. Restricted as the company was to enlarging the Giulia power unit, the way in which this was done suggested a step backwards rather than a step forwards, and a rather hesitant step at that.

First of all the bore diameter was enlarged from 78mm to 80mm. This fairly trifling increase was backed up by a three times larger addition to the stroke of the engine, taking it from 82mm to 88.5mm. Not only did this decrease the ratio of bore to stroke from the almost 'square' dimensions of the Giulietta and the rather more conservative proportions of the Giulia, but it gave an even lower bore-to-stroke ratio than on the original 1900.

These modest changes boosted the capacity from 1570cc to 1779cc. But the longer stroke meant that any increase in engine speed would increase the internal stresses, thus strictly limiting any resultant power increase. Even as it was, the alloy

cylinder block casting had to be strengthened to enable it to stand up to the increased loading. Otherwise, the car inherited the camshafts, manifolds and specification of the Giulia Super, with a 9:1 compression ratio and a pair of double-choke carburettors, although as with the Spider and coupé versions, cars intended for the American market were fitted with a completely new fuel-injection system.

There were to be three more major differences between the new range and its two immediate predecessors. First of all, the three versions of saloon, Bertone-bodied Sprint coupé and Spider would all be introduced at the same time. Second, they would all share the same engine tune and power output, without the two sporting models being given extra performance. Third, the idea of using names for the model range would be

Alfa devoutly hoped that the 1750s would follow in their ancestors' charismatic wheeltracks

dropped, and Alfa Romeo would return to the kind of numerical designation that had stood it in such good stead in the past.

The modest bore and stroke increases took the engine capacity to within a cupful or so of the 1752cc of one of the most beautiful, most charismatic and most successful Alfa Romeos of all time, the lovely 1750 of pre-war days. With a little bit of poetic, and mathematical, licence the title might be justifiable. So the new range was announced as the Alfa Romeo 1750s, and the company devoutly hoped they would follow in their ancestors' wheeltracks.

1750 Berlina
1967–1972

ENGINE:
Four-cylinder, twin ohc
Bore x stroke	80 x 88.5mm
Capacity	1779cc
Power	118bhp

TRANSMISSION:
Five-speed gearbox
Final drive	4.556:1

BODY STYLE:
Four-door saloon

PERFORMANCE:
(from contemporary sources)
Max speed	117mph (187kph)
0–60mph (97kph)	10.8 seconds

LENGTH:	14ft 5in (4.39m)
WIDTH:	5ft 1.7in (1.56m)
WHEELBASE:	8ft 5in (2.57m)

2000 Berlina
1971–76

As 1750 Berlina, except:
ENGINE:
Four-cylinder, twin ohc
Bore x stroke	84 x 88.5mm
Capacity	1,962cc
Power	132bhp

TRANSMISSION:
Five-speed gearbox
Final drive	4.556:1

BODY STYLE:
Four-door saloon

PERFORMANCE:
(from contemporary sources)
Max speed	118mph (189kph)
0–60mph (97kph)	9.7 seconds

NUMBER BUILT:
1750 Berlina	101,880 approx
2000 Berlina	89,840

This cutaway drawing of the 1750
Berlina reveals the clear line of
mechanical ancestry – from the four-
cylinder twin-cam engine to the
carefully located rigid rear axle – that
stretched right back to the Alfa 1900.
(Alfa Romeo archives)

The Spider was the least changed,
anyway initially, simply inheriting the
larger engine in the body, chassis and
running gear of the Duetto. The 1750
GTV also took over from the Giulia
GTV in the same business-as-usual
way. This time it was the saloon that
showed the most obvious differences
from its immediate predecessor,
although it still had a strong family
resemblance. The design had been
entrusted to Bertone, who carried out
an extremely skilful reworking of the
original Satta box into a much more
modern shape.

The dimensions of the 1750 Berlina
were almost identical to those of its
Giulia predecessor. The front and rear
track were identical, and the
wheelbase was stretched by 2 inches
(5cm). Yet by lengthening the body by
almost 10 inches, it was possible to
provide more space for the rear seat
passengers. Equally, by merely

softening the edges of the boxy
shape, particularly over the front and
rear wings, cleaning up the design of
the Kamm tail, and fitting a new,
broader radiator shield, flanked by
paired headlamps, Bertone
succeeded in making the car look
quite new, and appreciably larger
than was implied by the modest
change in actual size.

There were sound practical
advantages to the new design.
Underbonnet room was increased,
making engine accessibility easier,
and at the opposite end of the car
there was more room for luggage in
the larger boot. Inside, the car had a
touch more luxury than its
predecessors. The driver faced a pair
of cowled instruments set behind the
dished steering wheel, whose three
polished-alloy spokes incorporated
black plastic horn buttons. The other
instruments were set in a centre
console sweeping back from beneath

RIGHT:
Rear view of the 1750 Berlina. The car's
derivation from the Giulia is clear. (LAT)

The interior of the 1750 was more lavishly finished than the Giulia, with a wooden-rimmed steering wheel (and a wood-finish boss in the centre!), a wooden strip across the dash, heavily cowled main instruments, and the auxiliary dials grouped in the centre console. (Alfa Romeo archives)

the dash to between the two front bucket seats. Elsewhere, wood finish replaced painted metal, and soft carpets replaced rubber mats, in a definite move towards satisfying a progressively more demanding market.

The penalty for all this change was an appreciable increase in body weight over that of the Giulia TI. The difference amounted to 3cwt (150kg), which absorbed much of the engine's extra power of 135bhp at 5,800rpm, although top speed crept up a whisker to just over 112mph (180kph) and acceleration was slightly improved, together with flexibility in each gear, thanks to the increase in torque.

Alfa Romeo's prospects depended on how well the car appealed to its

traditional customers. On the basis of the road-test coverage, it promised to do well. In Britain Autocar tested the 1750 Berlina and found that the engine did its job as well as ever in this new, enlarged version. 'There is never any fuss or bother from this highly tuned sports engine,' reported the magazine, '. . . it pulls smoothly and evenly from idling right up past the start of the red line at 6,000rpm.' The writer referred to 'a mellow blend of cams, chains, induction and exhaust which never rises above the pleasing, muted roar even at maximum revs' and summed the car up as 'one of the most relaxed high-speed cruisers we have come across.'

This was the kind of opinion that Alfa undoubtedly wanted to hear. But there were other criticisms of the new design that are worth bearing in mind today. One consequence of the larger engine and the revised chassis was a shift of weight towards the front end of the car. If anything, this tended to

'There is never any bother from the 1750 Berlina's highly tuned sports engine'

increase the Alfa tendency towards mild understeer, although as before the steering proved to be lively and responsive. At its limits, the car tended to lift the inside front wheel rather than the rear one, but cornering was stable and clearly the basic suspension system was still

doing its duty on these bigger, heavier and more opulent models.

The servo-assisted brakes were a little too much of a good thing on some of the cars, until drivers learned to use gentler pressure on the pedal. As with some of the earlier models, however, it was the driving position that came in for most criticism. The seats were comfortable enough, but drivers were unhappy with the pedals, which were pivoted under the floor and set at an angle that some drivers found uncomfortable to operate. The new dash layout was a mixed blessing. There was no question that the speedometer and tachometer were clear, easy to read and sensibly placed, but the subsidiary instruments on the centre console tended to be

obscured by the steering wheel and column control stalks.

In this move upmarket, Alfa would also have to address another, and much more serious, problem. In the old days the company's products – even the 1900 – had been put together with the care and attention of skilled craftsmen. With the Giulietta and Giulia the production rate had shot skywards, and with it the number of complaints from customers about poor finish and, in a few cases, poor reliability. Although most customers were probably

Another deliciously stylised PR shot of the 1750; note the narrow Alfa shield on the grille. (Alfa Romeo archives)

Competition 1750s

In one respect at least, the 1750 lived up to an earlier and well-established Alfa Romeo tradition. In July 1968, just six months after the range had first been shown to the press at Vietri sul Mare near Salerno, a quartet of 1750 Berlinas was entered for the 24-hour Race at Spa-Francorchamps in Belgium. By now enough of the cars had been made for the design to be homologated for racing in the Group One production tourer category, and they emulated a whole string of production car Alfa victories of the past by finishing in first, second, third and fourth overall in their class. Another 1750 finished first in the production touring car class in the 1968 Coupe des Alpes. And all this was taking place when the GTAs were notching up wins in events all over Europe, Africa and South America!

perfectly happy with their cars, and with the service they had from the company and its agents, the minority who were not could have a severe effect on continuing sales. And it was already clear that the 1750 range also had its share of problems in this respect.

Other problems related to the changes made between the Giulia and the 1750 in particular. The increase in power and torque threw greater stress on the clutch, which had already begun to show weaknesses on earlier models. The 1750 version was still a single dry-plate unit, as it had been on the Giulia, but a series of modifications had to be made for it to cope with the higher stresses. In addition, the increased weight and speed of the car increased the demands made on the rear suspension under severe cornering, at a time when competitors' cars were relying increasingly on more sophisticated independent rear suspension systems.

For the moment, though, the sales figures were encouraging. In 1968 the total number of Giulias fell back to 55,168 for the year, but these were augmented by 42,114 of the new 1750s, taking the company's total output to a high of 97,282. In the following year, 1969, production of the 1750s fell back to a total of just 36,568 units, but the figures for the years after that went on rising by around 5 per cent a year.

By 1970, although sales of the 1750s were increasing, due to the falling-off of Giulia production the company's overall output actually declined. In the meantime, all three cars in the range had a comprehensive facelift. In the case of the 1750 Berlina, this involved revised pedals of the pendant type, operating in a more comfortable arc, a new steering wheel that was more deeply dished than its predecessor, quartz-iodine headlamps, and a dual-circuit braking system.

Increasing the engine size had put Alfa Romeo in a cleft stick. An arcane formula was used to determine road tax in Italy: this involved multiplying the number of cylinders by 0.08782, then multiplying the answer by the engine's capacity in cubic centimetres raised to the power 0.6541, to produce a notional figure for its power output. This decided the amount of tax to be paid, and it had the effect that Italian drivers paid more road tax for cars with capacities greater than the modest figure of 1500cc than anyone else in Europe. This in turn meant that Italians tended, in the main, to go for smaller cars. In 1967 the average capacity of German-owned cars was 1445cc, and of British-owned cars 1385cc; Italian-owned cars had an average capacity of 890cc.

So the 1750 was in danger of falling between two objectives. On the one hand its increased engine size frightened off less well-heeled customers because of the higher running costs, while the increase in power and performance was not enough to electrify those customers who wanted both, and had the means to pay for them. While the less well-off enthusiasts were still catered for by the Giulias and other smaller-engined cars, perhaps the top of the range needed still more treatment?

The answer, as so often in Alfa history, lay in the competition cars. Apart from the competition versions of the 1750 Berlina, the brunt of the company's racing programme had been borne by the redoubtable GTAs (see Chapter 8), now running in 1750 form. Since the most keenly contested class in adapted production-car racing for 1970 promised to be the 2-litre class, Autodelta set to work to develop the GTA 1750 to race in this division. For the first event in the 1970 European Touring Car Challenge, the Monza 4-Hour race, a car called the 1750 GTAm was entered for the first time. The 'm' in the designation stood for *maggiorata*, or enlarged, as the

engine cylinder bores had been enlarged from 80 to 84.5mm, taking the capacity to 1985cc.

The GTAm proved a resounding success, taking first place overall. It happened again at Zandvoort, at Budapest, at Montlhéry, at Dijon and a succession of other events, winning another Touring Car Challenge for Alfa Romeo in its very first season. It did it again a year later, with the engine now delivering 240bhp at 7,500rpm. It was all too clear that boosting capacity to a full 2 litres did no damage at all to the traditional strengths of the Alfa engine design, even under the stresses of racing.

So by June 1971 Alfa Romeo had applied the lessons of racing to its

production car programme – an enduring theme in the company's long history. Shown to the press at Gardone on Lake Garda was a trio of re-engined 1750s, now to be known as the 2000 Berlina, Spider and GTV. The treatment differed slightly from that used to produce the GTAm, in that the bores were enlarged to 84mm to avoid too tight a spacing between them. This raised the capacity to 1962cc, and the power, with the same compression ratio and carburation as before, increased to a peak of 132bhp at 5,500rpm.

Clearly the relatively longer stroke of the bigger engines was still having its effect on the top end of the speed range, since the power peak was occurring 1000rpm lower than it had

The 2000 saloon was almost identical to the 1750 from the outside, except for the wider Alfa shield at the front, and the inner pair of headlamps being set forward from the others with all four lamps now the same size. (Alfa Romeo archives)

The Alfa 2000 interior layout had even more wood trim spread around the dash and central console, but some found the white-on-black-on-white main instruments difficult to read. (Alfa Romeo archives)

on the Giulia SS, and 700rpm lower than on the Giulia TI. Nevertheless, the top speed of the 2000 saloon climbed to 118mph (190kph), and responsiveness over the entire speed range was improved.

In other respects the design was beginning to show its age. The clutch was modified to cope with increased power, and was increasingly heavy in its action. The nose-heavy tendency of the design was still more marked, with a consequent increase in understeer, and there were noticeable shortcomings in the synchromesh on some examples, particularly on the change into second gear.

In addition, some changes in detail design were definitely for the worse,

and seemed to indicate a change in the company's priorities. Over the years the instrumentation of all Alfas had been improving, and edging closer to meeting the driver's real needs. In the case of the 2000 Berlina, however, the two main dials were changed to a confusing set of white-on-black-on-white figures which were actually much harder to read than the ordinary white-on-black numerals, and which deserved some kind of award as the year's most pointless styling gimmick. Second, another change from 1971 seemed to symbolise the steepening decline in the company's confidence in its own ability to keep its loyal customers happy. For the makers of what had long been regarded as one of the best gearboxes in the world to

In profile, the unadorned lines of the 2000 – here with optional alloy wheels – seem almost too plain. (Alfa Romeo archives)

offer its performance-conscious buyers the option of an automatic box seemed to verge on the bizarre.

But for the time being, the 2000 would go on selling at more than 50,000 units a year. With a new small car in the pipeline to maintain the company's presence in that market, it was high time for new thinking at the top end of the market.

If contemplating a 1750 or 2000 Berlina today, it is understandable to think that these bigger models are just a shade too sizeable for their own good. But although there is a touch more roll, and a touch more understeer, in all other respects the ultimate Satta saloons retain the crisp sportiness expected of an Alfa, while offering family owners more space and a bigger boot.

The steering and gearbox are as incisive as ever, the levels of roadholding and handling much as those of the Giulia, and in addition you have a better – but still firm and well-controlled – ride that is most impressive for a car with a solid rear axle. The 1750, as would be expected, is more rev-happy, the 2000 more flexible – but even the bigger engine needs 2,500rpm on the clock before it really starts to come alive. The cars still sound like Alfas, too, with that twin-cam growl telling you that you have bought an Italian thoroughbred rather than a lazily cosseting Rover 2000 or six-cylinder Triumph.

Buying Hints

1. Body and mechanical checkpoints are as the Giulia saloon, from which these later cars were derived. As the cars have always had a limited following, expect a fair hunt to find one, and expect many to be in unloved condition.

2. Do not feel that the 1750 is a poor relation to the 2000. While the bigger-engined car benefits from its torquey 2-litre power unit, its interior is less pleasing than that of the 1750.

The Giulia, 1750 &
2000 *Bertone coupés*

A Sprint GT being followed by a 1750 GTV, identified by its quadruple headlamps and the single brightly finished horizontal bar across the front panel. (LAT)

When the Giulietta range had set Alfa Romeo on the road to true post-war recovery, the model that had appeared first was Bertone's Sprint coupé, and the Sprint had continued in production throughout the Giulietta's life span, surviving long enough to be fitted in 1962 with the 1570cc version of the company's classic twin-cam four-cylinder engine, to form part of the Giulia range. Its time finally came in the autumn of 1963, although it would continue in production for another two years in Giulietta-engined 1300 Sprint form.

On 9 September 1963 a new Bertone coupé design was unveiled to the Italian press at the company's new Arese works, and later at the Frankfurt Motor Show. Its very subtle redesign of the body shape made the

new car look very like a scaled-down 2600 coupé, with a higher roofline at the back, tapering down to a more streamlined tail. Although the wheelbase was just over an inch shorter, the reshaped body was more efficient aerodynamically, and provided more headroom in the rear, turning the car into a genuine four-seater.

This was the Giulia Sprint GT, and it was to become one of the best-loved Alfa designs of all. In its initial form it was fitted with twin double-choke carburettors and, with a 9:1 compression ratio, its 106bhp version of the 1570cc Giulia engine gave it a top speed of 112mph (180kph) and brisk acceleration. To make the most of the extra interior room, the rear seats were bigger and more deeply upholstered, and the doors were wider. The front seats were in cloth, with those parts likely to endure the hardest wear being faced in leather.

The raked rear screen made for a light and airy interior, although the fairly sharp curvature produced a degree of distortion when looking through the glass. Floor coverings were carpet, with plastic mats for heavy-wear areas. The only interior

The Giulia Sprint GT was to become one of the best-loved Alfa designs of all

storage space was provided by a small lockable cubby-hole in the dashboard, and a recess for maps and papers. Instruments included a matching tachometer and speedometer in front of the driver, while a cluster of secondary instruments for fuel, water and oil temperatures and oil pressure were set on the driver's side of the dashboard. The boot lid was released

Giulia Sprint GT/GT Veloce 1963–1968

ENGINE:
Four-cylinder, twin ohc
Bore x stroke	78 x 82mm
Capacity	1570cc

Power	106bhp (Veloce 109bhp)
Max speed	112mph (180kph)
Veloce	115mph (185kph)
0–60mph (97kph)	10.6 seconds;
Veloce	10.5 seconds

LENGTH:	13ft 5in (4.09m)
WIDTH:	5ft 2in (1.57m)
WHEELBASE:	7ft 9in (2.36m)

1750 Sprint GTV 1967–1972

As Giulia Sprint GT except:
ENGINE:
Capacity	1779cc
Power	118bhp

PERFORMANCE:
(from contemporary sources)
Max speed	118mph (190kph)
0–60mph (97kph)	9.3 seconds

2000 GTV 1971–1976

As 1750 Sprint GTV except:
ENGINE:
Capacity	1962cc
Power	132bhp

PERFORMANCE:
(from contemporary sources)
Max speed	121mph (195kph)
0–60mph (97kph)	9.1 seconds

Montreal 1971–1977

ENGINE:
Eight cylinders in vee, quad–cam
Bore x stroke	80 x 64.5mm
Capacity	2593cc
Power	200bhp

TRANSMISSION:
Five-speed ZF
Final drive	4.10:1
Limited–slip differential	

BODY STYLE:
Two-door 2+2 coupé

PERFORMANCE
(from contemporary sources)
Max speed	136mph (219kph)
0–60mph (97kph)	7.5 seconds

LENGTH:	13ft 11in (4.22m)
WIDTH:	5ft 6in (1.67m)
HEIGHT:	4ft 11in (1.21m)

NUMBER BUILT:
GT 1300 Junior	91,195
GT 1600 Junior Z	402
GT 1300 Junior Z	1,108
GT 1600 Junior	14.299
GTA 1300	447
Giulia Sprint GT	21,542
Giulia Sprint GT Veloce	14,240
Giulia GTA	500
1750 Sprint GTV	44,265
2000 GTV	37,459
1750 GTAm/2000 GTAm	40
Montreal	3,925

Inside the Giulia Sprint GTV, with its mock wood dashboard, instruments set in front of the driver, dished steering wheel with the horn buttons in the polished alloy spokes, and the long gear lever controlling the beautifully precise change. (Alfa Romeo archives)

the lever towards the central, third–fourth plane, so that changes from second up to third could be accomplished just by pushing the lever forward and letting the springs guide it into the right slot. In the same way, dropping down from fifth to fourth for a brisker response at speed meant pulling back on the lever, and leaving it to the spring bias to slot it neatly into position.

Noise was becoming something of a problem: in overdrive fifth, the exhaust boom was loud enough to be noticeable. In addition, a wind whistle round the windows or the opening rear quarterlights could be very difficult to eradicate. Road noise varied with the tyres, and was intrusive over really poor surfaces.

In terms of roadholding the Giulia Sprint GT was just as good as its stablemates, which meant very good indeed. Thanks to a strong and carefully set-up front suspension, and a live rear axle as precisely located as any in the business, its handling was top-class. When Alfa first designed the set-up for the Giulietta, the prototypes were fitted with suspension settings calculated to produce differing amounts of understeer and oversteer, and competition drivers carried out road tests. The consensus of opinion was that the most comfortable handling from all points of view was a mild degree of understeer, and this setting was used on all subsequent Alfas, including the Sprint GT.

from a lockable handle recessed into the passenger door rear pillar.

All this extra trim and equipment inside the car, plus the new bodywork, conspired to increase the weight by 100lb (45kg). The car was still relatively brisk in acceleration, although the engine really came into its own past the 60mph mark. However, it was essential to use the gearbox to the full to keep the free-revving engine in the right part of its speed range.

Fortunately, as with all the five-speed Alfas, the gearchange was a joy. The spring bias system tended to push

The Sprint GT was the first Alfa to be assembled in the new Arese works, even though the mechanicals still came from the original Portello factory. Although the car was appreciably more expensive than the Sprint coupé that it replaced, its sales soon began to take off. Just over 7,000 of the final 1570cc version of the earlier design, called the Sprint 1600, were sold in two years of production. By contrast, the Sprint GT sold three times this figure in just three years. It became the most popular model in the Giulia range, and the most popular Alfa of its time on the UK market.

In 1963, its first year of production, 848 were sold. But in 1964 10,839 Sprint GTs emerged from the factory, no fewer than 960 of them being right-hand-drive cars. In 1965 the figures dropped slightly, to a total of 10,053, including 651 right-hand-drive cars, then in 1966 fell away entirely, to a total of 162, of which 29 had right-hand-drive.

In 1965, as the Giulia Sprint Speciale finally ceased production, a very different version of the Giulia Sprint GT emerged to tempt buyers looking for something different. This was the Giulia Sprint GTC, a convertible version designed by Carrozzeria Touring, which offered four seats and a completely folding hood in a car that still managed to make the most of Bertone's elegant lines.

The production arrangements were, however, complex. The Bertone Sprint GT bodies were now made at Alfa Romeo's new plant at Arese in the countryside outside Milan, and those selected for the Touring treatment had to be taken off the line and sent to the latter's workshop for extra bracing to be added, the roofs cut off and the hoods fitted. It was moderately successful in production terms for a small concern, with a thousand of the cars sold for almost the same price as the Giulia SS.

The success of the Sprint GT moved Alfa to introduce a better and more powerful version, the Sprint GT Veloce, or GTV, and this became even more popular, and one of the Alfa Romeo all-time greats. It was launched simultaneously with the new 1600 Spider (the future Duetto) in March 1966. Members of the motoring press were invited to try the car out on a 44-mile (70km) road circuit along the edge of Lake Garda, through the neighbouring mountains and along a stretch of autostrada.

This was a cunning piece of news management on the company's part, since the overriding virtue of the GTV was that it was such an excellent compromise between the requirements of these markedly different driving environments.

On paper, the differences between the Sprint GT and the GTV were not great. The compression ratio was the

Also based on the Giulia chassis was this Touring-built cabriolet, sold as the Giulia Sprint GTC, which offered buyers the increasingly rare option of a once-common species, the four-seater open tourer. (LAT)

The neat rear-end treatment of the Bertone Sprint GT design, shown to advantage on this immaculate 1750 GTV. (LAT)

interior trim and other detail changes were between them responsible for raising the car's overall weight by no less than 1.4cwt (70kg).

In reality, the car's appeal was a case of the whole being more than merely the sum of its parts. Whatever a simple comparison of the figures might have suggested, there was always something about a well-set-up GTV that provided such a balanced combination of room, style, performance, handling and all-round responsiveness that its appeal was instant, and enduring. For a long and demanding journey with every kind of road condition, it was ideal. For once, the GTV's capabilities made the GT tag entirely appropriate.

A total of 6,901 GTVs were produced in 1966, including 583 right-hand-drive cars, which seemed a promising beginning. In 1967 production actually fell away slightly, with 6,541 cars produced in all, 822 of them right-hand-drive. In 1968 just 27 left-hand-drive and a pair of right-hand-drive GTVs were made, as the GTV gave way to a more powerful 1750 version, launched alongside the new 1750 Berlina and Spider. The 1750 GTV shared their 118bhp (132bhp gross) variant of the bored-and-stroked 1779cc version of the classic twin overhead-cam 'four'. Outwardly the 1750 GTV was much the same as its predecessor, except that there was now only one chromed grille bar, and an extra pair of headlamps at the front. In addition, the oddly stepped front-end treatment of the Giulia Sprint GT and GTV, together with the GT Junior, where the bonnet lid panel was raised above the top of the car's nose, was now tidied up into a neater flush-fitting configuration. The weight crept up again by just 44lb (20kg), but the speed crept up as well, to 118mph (190kph).

Motor tried the new version in July 1968. 'Testing the Alfa Romeo 1750 GT Veloce was rather like meeting an old friend – a friend improved in

same, as was the carburation, and the peak horsepower climbed by just 3bhp to 109bhp, increasing the top speed by just over 3mph (5kph) to 115mph (185kph). The only differences apparent from the outside were a revised set of three chrome grille bars on the front of the car, the addition of the word 'Veloce' to the chrome script at the back, and a discreet metal four-leaf clover badge, the emblem of the old Alfa Corse works racing team, on each of the rear quarter pillars. Inside, the front seats were reshaped to provide more comfort and support. More significantly, the increased level of

Junior Zagato

At the opposite end of the spectrum from the Montreal, in 1969 Zagato produced another variation on the production Alfa Romeo floorpan and running gear to fill the gap left by the last of the Tubolares. This was the exquisitely styled but rather poorly named GT1300 Junior Z, which sounded like some poor relation of an existing model but was in fact an entirely new design. By fitting the Giulietta engine and the five-speed gearbox into a body built up on the Zagato space-frame construction for lightness and strength, the Junior Z not only looked good, but also went well, with 89bhp driving an all-up weight of 18cwt (920kg). Its top speed was 109mph (175kph), with

lines sweeping upwards and backwards from a drooped nose to an elegantly curving window line, ending in a sloping fastback with an opening rear hatch and a Kamm tail.

Other features of the design included a transparent panel at the front end enclosing the headlamps, with a central air-intake aperture in the form of the traditional Alfa shield. Because the car was built in Zagato's workshops relatively few were made, and most of those were sold on the home market. In all 1,108 were produced by the end of 1972, when the original design was replaced by a version fitted with the 1570cc engine as used in the Duetto and the original

GTV, and having detailed alterations in the form of larger bumpers and revised trim. This remained in production for another three years, but only 402 of the larger-engined cars were made. One reason for the small production might have been the price, which was almost as high as the 2000 GTV.

Zagato's Junior Z was individualistically styled but its high price meant barely 1500 were made, over a six-year life. (LAT)

status and prosperity,' it began. 'This is not so much due to familiarity, although it is the fifth Alfa to come under our scrutiny in four years, but because once more the general excellence of these Italian cars has been brought home to us.'

The testers also commented on the quietness of the car, even when using its performance to the full, thanks to the improved sound insulation that

probably contributed to the overall weight gain. But they came close to encapsulating the whole appeal of cars like the GTV when they described how thoroughly it vanquished bigger and more powerful opposition. 'In a week spent on give-and-take Belgian and French roads in the company of an American sports car of four times the capacity and three times the power . . . the Alfa was seldom left far behind, and on

Interior of the 1750 GTV – a more pleasing environment than in the later 2000 GTV. (LAT)

comfortable ride provided even on some of the worst roads to be found in Belgium: concave in cross section and covered with ruptured pavé, these make the roughest British roads seem as flat as plate glass by comparison.' Just about the only points of criticism were the driving position for taller drivers, since the magazine found the steering wheel a little too far away and the pedals too close, the restricted legroom in the rear seats, and a persistent flat spot near 2,000rpm.

Autocar tested the car two months later and noted that the engine speeds were limited to 6,000rpm as a consequence of the longer stroke,

'The firmness of the ride gives a pleasantly taut feel to the 1750 GTV'

where previously they had run to over 7,000rpm without harm. Nevertheless, wrote the magazine, 'all who drove the Alfa Romeo 1750 GTV were tremendously impressed by it. Compared with the 1600 version we tested in December 1966 it felt a whole lot livelier, with even better steering, handling and brakes, and a much nicer interior.' Although the lower engine speed limit meant that the testers could detect no improvement in acceleration through the gears, they were surprised to find that the bigger car was undeniably more economical than the 1600 GTV, with a test average of 23.9mpg compared with 21.9mpg in the previous test. At a steady speed of 80mph (128kph) the 1750 GTV used fuel at the same rate (27mpg) as the 1600 GTV had used at 70mph (112kph).

The testers liked the steering but were not so impressed with the ride, as 'at low speeds the suspension is rather firm, and transmits a lot of

rough, twisty roads it could often go faster.'

The maintenance of excellent handling in what was now a heavier, more powerful and faster car was due to careful detail changes to the suspension settings. These included modifications to the geometry of the front wishbones to raise the roll centre. This lessened the tendency to roll on the entrance to a bend, but also tended to produce more weight transfer to the front of the car, which was then partly counteracted by fitting slightly softer front springs. The rear suspension was fitted with an anti-roll bar, and the wheels were made smaller and wider in section.

The results were a continuation of the Alfa properties of mild, stable understeer to give what *Motor* described as 'superb – perhaps better – roadholding'. Ride comfort, too, was praised in superlative terms: 'A remarkable feature was the joggy reaction over poor roads', but they went on to say that 'the firmness of the ride gives a pleasantly taut feel to the car'. On the other hand, they did not find the seats as comfortable as their appearance suggested, although they did not seem to find any engine flat spots, and as always the handling and the gearbox came in for high praise. Once again their summing-up helps to explain the enduring appeal of this particular model, when they admitted that 'the extra engine capacity has made it more economical and although performance is not materially affected, the car is far more responsive and eager than before. It is very fast, has a high safety factor, and is fun to drive.'

Production of the 1750 GTV began in 1967, with 919 having emerged from the Arese plant by the end of the year. In 1968 11,768 1750 GTVs were produced, including 1,082 of the right-hand-drive version, out of a total year's 1750 series output of 42,114 cars. Next year, following the apparently usual pattern, output dropped a fraction to 10,799 GTVs, including 1,454 right-hand-drive cars. In 1970 output climbed more sharply to a total of 13,973 GTVs, including 1,452 right-hand-drive cars, but this was to be the model's best year.

A competition version of the Giulia Sprint GT also appeared; with bodywork in light alloy, and sound deadening and other creature comforts removed, the weight was reduced by 4cwt (205kg), this being the reason for its being renamed the GTA, for *Gran Turismo Allegerita* (or 'lightened'). With twin-ignition engines in varying states of tune, delivering power outputs between 115 and 170bhp, and top speeds of between 115mph and 137mph

A Sprint GTA in the foreground, with a 2000 GTV behind. (LAT)

The functional but not completely spartan interior of a well-preserved right-hand-drive GTA. (LAT)

ordinary fuel mixtures, with additional cooling provided by water injection through the inlet manifold. The GTA-SA (for *Sovralimentata* or 'Supercharged') was intended for Group 5 Touring Car races, and was timed at a top speed of 150mph (240kph) at the company test track. The real benefit was acceleration, which helped the car to win the Hockenheim 100-mile race outright in 1967, followed by four more outright wins during the 1968 season.

Finally, between 1968 and 1972 447 more GTAs were produced with a 1290cc engine. Although the engines had the same capacity as the Giulietta, they were in fact a larger-bore, shorter-stroke oversquare version with twin ignition producing 96bhp in basic form. This was soon increased to 110bhp, pushing up the top speed from 109mph (175kph) to 130mph (275kph), but the Autodelta versions were already delivering a resounding 160bhp at 7,800rpm. Even more exotic were 100 fuel-injected cars prepared by Autodelta and delivering 165bhp at 8,400rpm, a remarkable tribute to the strength and efficiency of an engine design dating back several decades.

In the meantime, Alfa had also been continuing to cater for purchasers unable to afford the buying and running costs of the Sprint GTs by turning out the usual smaller-engined version of the GT, principally for the home market. This was the Alfa GT1300 Junior, introduced in 1966 and powered by the old, almost 'square' Giulietta engine with the same carburettors and compression ratio as the larger cars, but in this case delivering 89bhp net (103bhp gross) at 6,000rpm. The car was also 2.2cwt (110kg) lighter than the 1750 GTV, at 18.3cwt (930kg) overall, and it had a top speed of 106mph (170kph). It sold in Italy for about three-quarters of the price of the 1750 GTV, cost less to tax and used less fuel, and in eleven years of production more than 90,000 were produced, of which more than

(185kph and 220kph), the GTAs swept all before them. For three seasons, from 1966 to 1968, they won for Alfa Romeo three successive European Manufacturers Challenges and a string of national championships.

Five hundred of the cars were made for sale, plus an unspecified number for the Autodelta team, and ten more with twin centrifugal superchargers, powered from a hydraulic pump chain-driven from the engine. This allowed the car to be driven on

A GTA being driven in anger on the Circuit Paul Ricard in 1971. (Alfa Romeo archives)

4,500 were right-hand-drive. From 1972 a further model joined the range – a 1600cc GT Junior that effectively revived the original Giulia GT Sprint. Only 14,299 were made.

In 1967 the centenary of the foundation of the Canadian Federation was celebrated by the Montreal Expo, which featured all manner of new and exciting designs and products including, in the automotive category, a sleek Alfa Romeo coupé with 2+2 coupé bodywork by Bertone, based around a roadgoing version of the V8 engine designed for the Alfa 33 racing prototype. The bores were narrowed

from the 84mm of the 3-litre racing unit to 80mm, reducing the capacity to 2593cc, and the chassis and running gear of the car shown in Montreal were modified from the Giulia GTV.

Three years later the company put the car into limited production. Named the Montreal in honour of its first appearance, the body style bore no resemblance to any of the company's other models, nor did the engine design. With fuel injection and 9.3:1 compression ratio, the 2.6-litre V8 delivered 200bhp at 6,500rpm, giving a top speed of more than 132mph (220kph). From the beginning the Montreal was both rare and expensive. It cost twice as much as a GTV, and in seven years just under 4,000 were made. Nevertheless, the survivors remain highly prized collectors' items.

Are they worth it? The Montreal is all about the engine and the styling. Form your own opinion about Bertone's striking shell, but what of

The family of smaller-engined Alfas: 1300 Spider (note uncowled headlamps with painted rims), Giulia Super 1300 (with late type of grille), and GT1300 Junior (with the 2000 GTV style of grille found on the last of these cars). (Alfa Romeo archives)

The Montreal at speed. (LAT)

Daimler 2½-litre will know, there's a beguiling immediacy about small V8s, and the lack of cubic centimetres is definitely no hardship.

Performance is instant – and in all gears, thanks to a relatively low fifth – and the soundtrack melodious and hard-edged. Appropriately, the light and accurate gearchange is operated by a snappy stub of a lever rather than the slice-it-through long wand of other front-'box Alfas; first is on a limb, in typical ZF style, and the clutch is well weighted.

The chassis is less appealing: the balance that the 105 series underpinnings give to the Giulia saloon and more particularly to the GTVs is less apparent. Instead you get basinfuls of roll, and a fair dose of understeer, accompanied by a certain uneasiness on poor surfaces. Drive through this, and you can use the power to translate understeer into a more neutral pose. No – the Montreal, despite its glam looks, is no 1970s supercar, and its parts-bin

the race-bred quad-cam V8? It's not the temperamental beast you might expect, and in fact has all the smoothness, flexibility and sheer lugging power you would imagine a 200bhp V8 to offer – even if the displacement is nearly a litre below that of the disdainfully well-muscled but emphatically 'touring' Rover V8 unit. As lovers of the similarly sized

The beautiful Alfa Romeo Montreal, the exhibition car that became a collector's item. (LAT)

origins can make themselves felt. Better then to play *boulevardier* than boy racer with the Montreal: that, after all, is more in tune with the catwalk looks of Alfa's range-topping pretender.

During the course of 1971, in common with its two 1750 stablemates, the 1750 GTV left the stage. Its replacement was the 2000

'The 2000 GTV goes exactly where it is put in any corner'

GTV, which shared with the 2000 Berlina and Spider the same 132bhp 1962cc engine. Its weight was actually reduced by 1cwt (50kg) to 19.5cwt (990kg) and the engine's greater low-speed torque delivered better flexibility and a top speed of more than 121mph (195kph). Production was to continue until 1976, alongside the 1300 and 1600 sister cars described earlier.

There were a few detailed styling changes to go with the larger engine and change of model designation. The front end was revised, with the horizontal radiator grille bars being used to suggest the Alfa shield device. A subtle change to the line of the rear wings gave the car a slightly sleeker and more streamlined shape, and new seats and a revised dashboard inside the car provided a distinct improvement in driver comfort. The interior was now trimmed in chrome and vinyl, with all the instruments grouped in a panel behind the steering wheel, where the driver could scan them with the minimum of distraction from the road ahead.

Cars produced for the UK market were fitted with a limited-slip differential, to counter the tendency for the inner rear wheel to lift off the

road under hard cornering. The result was a great improvement in handling. 'The car goes exactly where it is put in any corner, and applying more or less power hardly changes the line at all, though up to a point the GTV feels more stable the more power is applied,' commented *Autocar*. With the limited-slip differential, it was possible to apply this useful extra power earlier in a corner, at the risk of reaching the car's ultimate limit, when it would show its impeccable balance by sliding sideways on all four wheels, under the influence of the immutable laws of physics.

Some details were less happy. For UK drivers the lines on the speedometer dividing each 10mph increment into three made monitoring of intermediate speeds a matter of mathematics rather than instant appraisal, and the arrangement of the dials on the central binnacle took some getting used to. On the other hand, after the problems of the late 1960s and early '70s, the finish of the cars did seem better, although long-term rustproofing would prove to be

such an enduring Achilles heel for the company that it would play a major role in its ultimate near-bankruptcy and final take-over.

Today the appeal of these cars is incontestable. Take the evolved mechanicals of the 105 series Giulia, wrap it in a taut-lined Bertone coupé body – in fact the work of one Giorgio Giugiaro – and you have the recipe for a seductive Italian that has had more than one respected journalist ask himself why anyone feels the need to bother with such a fickle mistress as a Ferrari.

Early Giulia GTs have a plain interior with a dummy-wood dash and rubber-mat flooring, giving an austerity to match their unadorned exterior. The driving experience is a step removed from that of later GTVs: the handling has the balance you'd expect, but the skinny rubber that means the car is less glued to the

High-speed luxury – the Montreal cockpit. (LAT)

A 2000 GTV at speed, identifiable by its revised front end, with the traditional Alfa shield being outlined only by raised sections of the radiator bars. (LAT)

road than a wider-wheeled 1750 or 2000, while the performance and refinement are clearly less impressive.

Step into a 1750 and you have a more opulent but still charismatic interior. Chrome, wood, cowled dials: it's a warming sight for any enthusiast. Less free-revving than the 1570cc unit, the longer-stroke 1750 is smoother and torquier, as well as more economical – no bad trade-off. As with all the 105 series coupés, roll is better controlled than on the taller saloons, and handling is gratifyingly precise. As speed mounts, so does the car's rapport with the driver: the steering lightens, communicating expressively all that is going on at the wheels, while the ride, firm at a pootle-along pace, smoothes out as you go faster. Similarly the clutch, heavy in traffic, seems just right when you're on the open road.

Of course you could come across one of the 1300 GT Junior models. With

the same well-honed chassis as the other coupés, the principal difference is in the way the small engine delivers its power. Less broad-shouldered in its flexibility, the 1290cc unit demands to be revved. In traffic you might feel handicapped, but out on country roads you can allow the car to come alive. As with all small-engined Alfas, this is a car that demands to be driven. Unsurprisingly,

a possible penalty is burnt-out exhaust valves, if you capitulate to the insistent charms of the willing little twin-cam.

Where does this leave the 2000 GTV? Is last-of-the-line best-of-the-bunch? Not from the interior, which seems contrived and somewhat down on quality. But out on the road the 2000 shines: beefy mid-range torque gives a relaxing flexibility when you need it, the limited-slip diff gives you more adhesion out of sharp corners, and the dual-circuit servo brakes are instantly reassuring. As a touring Alfa for tackling long distances in relaxed comfort, the 2000 has it over its lesser-engined siblings. For a mix of sweetness and egg-you-on insistence, however, the 1570cc Giulia Sprint and the 1750 GTV have a strong appeal, while take-no-prisoners drivers happy to keep the smallest of Alfa's twin-cams on the boil might appreciate the challenge offered by the 1300 Junior. Your choice . . .

The competition GTA (for *Allegerita*, or 'lightened') version of the GT Sprint, with extra frontal air intakes and lowered suspension. (LAT)

The Spider 4R Zagato

The Spider 4R Zagato arose from an idea put forward in the Italian motor magazine *Quattroruote* for a re-creation of the classic Alfa Romeo 1750s of the 1930s, using modern components. The car was built on the Giulia floorpan, with Giulia mechanicals, but the body at least was built by the old firm in the old way, and the car looked a great deal more genuine than many modern re-creations. With a screen that could be folded flat, cutaway doors and removable sidescreens and a hollow tail for luggage, it had much of the appeal of the original, and a comparable performance to the works supercharged cars of pre-war days. However, it cost as much as the Giulietta SS had done, was a great deal less practical, and only 92 were made between 1966 and 1968.

A shameful pastiche, or a worthwhile look back to the company's glory days? The Alfa Romeo *Quattroruote* Zagato 4R was based on the Giulia chassis and carried bodywork similar in style, if not in detail, to the classic two-seater of the late 1920s and early '30s. (LAT)

In its time the Sprint GT coupé in its different forms did the company proud. It sold well, earned the enduring loyalty of a whole generation of customers, and reams of solid praise from an otherwise increasingly cynical and outspoken motoring press. At the end of an article that pulled no punches in detailing some of the car's trivial shortcomings, *Car & Driver* paid it an eloquent tribute in its summing-up. The GTV, it wrote, 'hides nothing from you. You hear and *feel* the suspension and the tires working, your adrenaline pumps in almost direct proportion to the rise and fall in the exhaust note and the mechanical whirring of the double overhead camshafts' chain drive. At 4,000rpm you come to anticipate the sudden surge as the motor reaches towards its most efficient operating range. You're not driving a car, you're driving *with* it – a forceful and sometimes demanding partnership that is infinitely rewarding.'

The GTZ

Throughout its history Alfa Romeo relied heavily on the efforts of private owners to back up, and often replace, the company's own involvement in motor racing. When full-blooded racing machines were not on the agenda, the company would invariably make cars and components available in more competition-oriented form than the standard production version, or collaborate with other companies to produce more specialised combinations, such as the Giulietta SZ.

When the larger engine made the Sprint and Spider Giuliettas into Giulias overnight, the Giulietta SZ was one obvious exception. Instead of simply fitting the larger engine into the compact little coupé, Zagato went to work on a more thorough redesign, based on the later and more aerodynamically efficient version of the SZ.

This became the Giulia GTZ (Gran Turismo Zagato), which became universally known as the Tubolare; it was said that this was because of the tubular space frame that carried the body panels, but since that applied to every Zagato body made, it could also have been intended to describe the car's cross-section, which approximated to a circle, and which tapered back over the rear wheel-arches to end in a Kamm trefoil-shaped cut-off tail. It also had a coil-spring-and-wishbone independent rear suspension.

With light-alloy panelling and fixed plastic windows (opening quarter lights provided some ventilation), the GTZ turned the scales at a mere 12.8cwt (650kg). The basic production version was fitted with the same 112bhp version of the Giulia engine as the Bertone-bodied SS, which in this form gave it a top speed of 135mph (217kph) and a 0–60mph time of 7.5 seconds. In all, 112 of the cars were produced, qualifying it for GT racing, and in 1964 alone the Tubolares notched up class wins in races such as the Sebring 12 Hours, the Tour de France, the Targa Florio, the Le Mans 24 Hours, the Coupe des Alpes and the Tour de Corse.

RIGHT:
The extended-tail treatment of the later SZ was carried a stage further by Zagato for the Giulia GTZ Tubolare. (Alfa Romeo archives)

The Tubolare's development coincided with the re-establishment of a works racing effort, in the form of the Autodelta organisation. By 1965 the programme was sufficiently advanced for Autodelta to sponsor a series of 12 updated Tubolare TZ2s, with a lowered and reshaped body with glassfibre panelling, and much hotter engines featuring an 11.4:1 compression ratio, twin-plug ignition, and 170bhp, a prescription that secured the concern a long list of class wins in events all over Europe.

The sleek streamlining of the Tubolare (right) gave way in 1965 to the much more aggressive lines of the TZ2 (below). (Alfa Romeo archives)

With its simpler grille and plain large-diameter hubcaps the 1750 GTV has an air of quiet good breeding. This was somehow slightly dissipated in the later 2000 GTV. (LAT)

Buying Hints

Bertone coupés

1. The later coupés have a propensity to rust fully in proportion to their beautiful lines. Approach tatty or restoration-project cars with extreme caution and a robust constitution. Fortunately, a reasonable selection of repair sections is available.

2. Underneath, check the front chassis legs where they join the bulkhead and – as with the Giulia and 1750/2000 Berlinas – the front crossmember under the radiator. Moving inside, the footwells can hole near the front jacking points.

3. The front valance, the bottom of the front and rear wings, the rear valance, the door bottoms, the rear wheelarches, the sills: these are all predictably rust-prone. As on the earlier style of Sprint and on the Duetto/Spider, the shield intended to protect the A-posts and the rear of the front wings can harbour road dirt, causing bad corrosion at these points.

4. Further to this, the coupés rot around the front and rear screens, and the inner door frames (which are not easy to refabricate) also rust badly; adding piquancy, the door handles can drop out as the surrounding metal succumbs to tin-worm.

5. The bootlid is likely to have suffered from rust, and the spare-wheel well rots.

6. Mechanical failings are largely as on the Giulia saloons (so watch out for defective brakes on cars with dual-circuit systems), but note that in addition the rear springs are inclined to soften, leading to rear-end sag. Hard driving is also likely to have knocked out the dampers, while the bushes for the rear radius arms and the axle-locating T-bracket may have softened or worn. These last points, while possibly more likely on the coupés and Spiders, apply also to Giulia and 1750/2000 saloons.

7. For some reason early 1750s seem more prone to head-gasket problems caused by the cylinder liners slipping.

8. Interior trim items, including rubber matting (where fitted), are available from the original Italian supplier.

9. Replacement headlamps for the GT Junior and the 1750 and 2000 GTVs are difficult to source – the repro items available are not correct.

Montreal

1. Despite its limited production, the Montreal is not as rare as might be thought. In fact, with 100–130 survivors in the UK it is more common than certain more prosaic mass-production Alfas. Approximately half the UK-domiciled cars are left-hand-drive.

2. Don't be frightened by the thought of a race-bred V8 power unit: the Montreal's engine is low-stressed and long-lived. In any case, most cars have covered a relatively low mileage. Spares are not a problem, whatever rumours to the contrary you may have heard.

3. The gearbox is a robust ZF unit, shared with the Sunbeam-Lotus and 'droop-snoot' Vauxhall Firenza, amongst other cars.

4. The mechanicals are susceptible to sensitive uprating, and you may come across cars with BMW four-pot front brakes, Harvey-Baillie suspension kits and reworked electronic ignition. The Montreal Register of the Alfa Romeo OC is a fount of information on modernising your Montreal.

5. The mechanical fuel injection is vulnerable to inexpert attention, but need not pose problems if properly set up.

6. The chassis is 105 series Giulia; all parts are available.

7. Sills, wheelarches and lower wings are typical corrosion black-spots. The Montreal Register has sourced repair panels, and front wings are being re-made.

8. Most UK cars are known to the Montreal Register, and the Register is happy to look over a potential purchase for you. So join the club before opening your chequebook!

Alfa Romeo
Alfasud

By the early 1970s Alfa Romeo's engineering and production development had produced a series of models in a straight and unmistakable line of descent from the 1900 to the 2000, by way of the Giulietta, the Giulia and the 1750. Yet at the very time when the last in this splendid series was beginning to find acceptance with customers, another Alfa Romeo was about to make its appearance, and one that would start by apparently turning its back on every one of the company's hallowed engineering traditions.

Austrian engineer Rudolf Hruska certainly justified his salary, with an inspired design for a smaller front-drive Alfa. The use of a flat-four engine appeared to be a logical progression from his work at VW, even if it was fitted at the opposite end of the car. But the design of the engine

The original Alfasud saloon, with four doors and a boot, and an almost complete absence of embellishment. (Alfa Romeo archives)

Alfasud
1972–1976

ENGINE:
Four-cylinder, horizontally opposed
Bore x stroke   80 x 59mm
Capacity   1186cc
Power   63bhp

TRANSMISSION:
Four-speed gearbox
Final drive: 4.11:1

BODY STYLE:
Four-door saloon

PERFORMANCE:
(from contemporary sources)
Max speed   91mph (150kph)
0–60mph (97kph)   15.5 seconds

LENGTH: 12ft 9.2in (3.89m)

WIDTH: 5ft 2.6in (1.54m)

WHEELBASE: 8ft 0.6in (2.45m)

Alfasud TI
1974–78

As Alfasud Berlina except:
Five-speed gearbox
Max speed   100mph (160kph)
0–60mph (97kph)   14.2 seconds

BODY STYLE:
Two-door saloon

Alfasud 5m
1976–78

As Alfasud Berlina except:
Five-speed gearbox
Max speed   93mph (149kph)
0–60mph (97kph)   17.1 seconds

Alfasud 1300 Super
1977–79

As Alfasud Berlina except:
Bore x stroke   80 x 64mm
Capacity   1286cc
Power   68bhp
Five-speed gearbox
Max speed   98mph (157kph)
0–60mph (97kph)   12.8 seconds

Alfasud 1300 TI
1977–78

As Alfasud TI except:
Bore x stroke   80 x 64mm
Capacity   1286cc
Power   76bhp
Max speed   103mph (165kph)
0–60mph (97kph)   11.7 seconds

Alfasud Sprint 1.3
1977–1978

As Alfasud 1300TI except:
BODY STYLE: 2+2 closed coupé

LENGTH: 12ft 11in (3.94m)

WIDTH: 5ft 3.8in (1.62m)

Alfasud Super 1.3
1978–83

As Alfasud 1300 Super except:
Bore x stroke   80 x 67.2mm
Capacity   1351cc
Power   79bhp
Max speed   98mph (157kph)
0–60mph (97kph)   12.8 seconds

Alfasud Super 1.5
1978–1983

As Alfasud Super 1.3 except:
Bore x stroke   84 x 67.2mm
Capacity   1,490cc
Power   84bhp
Max speed   102mph (165kph)
0–60mph (97kph)   11.7 seconds

Alfasud Sprint 1.5
1978–79

As Alfasud Sprint 1.3 except:
Bore x stroke   84 x 67.2mm
Capacity   1490cc
Power   85bhp
Max speed   103mph (165kph)
0–60mph (97kph)   11.4 seconds

Alfasud 1.5 Sprint Veloce
1979–1983

As Alfasud Sprint 1.5 except:
Power   95bhp
Max speed   105mph (168kph)
0–60mph (97kph)   10.8 seconds

Alfasud Sprint Green Cloverleaf
1983–84

As Alfasud Sprint 1.5 Veloce except:
Power   105bhp
Max speed   115mph (185kph)
0–60mph (97kph)   10.3 seconds

Alfasud TIX 1.5
1983–84

As Alfasud 1300 TI except:
Bore x stroke   84 x 67.2mm
Capacity   1490cc
Power   95bhp
Max speed   108mph (173kph)
0–60mph (97kph)   10.1 seconds

LENGTH: 13ft 0.6in (3.98m)

WIDTH: 5ft 3.6in (1.62m)

Note: These body dimensions apply to all the hatchback versions of the saloons and TIs from 1981 to 1983, other parts of the specification remaining unchanged.

NUMBER BUILT:
Alfasud saloon, 5m,
1300 Super, Super 1.3,
Super 1.5   715,170

Alfasud TI, 1300 TI,
TIX 1.5   185,665

Alfasud Sprint 1.3,
Sprint 1.5, 1.5 Sprint Veloce,
Sprint Green Cloverleaf 102,053
                         (all to 3/84)

Neat and functional, the interior of the original Alfasud had no obvious associations with the rest of the range, nor did it hint at the car's considerable handling and performance potential. (Alfa Romeo archives)

fed by a lone single-choke carburettor mounted above the power unit and connected to the cylinders through a four-branch inlet manifold. With an 8.8:1 compression ratio, the engine in its initial form delivered a peak power output of 73bhp net (83bhp gross).

The power was harnessed to a four-speed all-synchro gearbox mounted, together with the diaphragm clutch and the differential, in an aluminium casing, split along its centre line and mounted behind the engine. A long extension fastened to the rear of this casting carried the rearmost engine support.

Based on a design by Giugiaro, the Alfasud's body was light and compact, incorporating a rigid central passenger cell with strong side

It was clear that the Alfasud was a very successful design indeed

members and a stiff central backbone. Because of the use of the flat-four engine, the bonnet line was kept low for good aerodynamics. The laminated windscreen was bonded to the body to take its share of the stresses, and there were crumple zones front and rear. In addition, the mass of the engine and transmission was intended to absorb high amounts of impact energy before intruding into the passenger compartment.

Deep transverse box sections helped ensure adequate body stiffness. One at the front, between the rear of the engine compartment and the dashboard, was known to the engineers as the 'bathtub' because of its shape, and helped brace the structure against twisting loads in between the front suspension mountings. Another deep box section at the rear between the back

owed little to established Alfa practice, with a single belt-driven overhead camshaft for each pair of cylinders, each operating a single row of valves opening into the combustion chamber roofs.

Another departure from VW practice was the use of water cooling, and the engine had very oversquare proportions, with an 80mm bore and a 59mm stroke, giving a capacity of 1186cc with low peak piston speeds. The crankcase and the two cylinder blocks were made from a single iron casting, the three-bearing crankshaft being fitted through an opening in the bottom of the engine.

Light alloy Heron-type cylinder heads were used, with combustion chamber spaces machined into the top of the slipper-type pistons. The cam belts and alternator belt were mounted at the front of the engine, with the gear-driven oil pump and distributor mounted at the back. The engine was seat and the boot provided further stiffness.

Twin-circuit brakes were an additional safety feature, with one circuit operating all four wheels, and the other the front wheels only, so that a minimum of 70 per cent of full braking effort was guaranteed under any circumstances of brake failure. The handbrake operated on the front wheels.

The car's front suspension used inclined MacPherson struts, semi-trailing lower wishbones and an anti-roll bar, with the disc brakes mounted inboard. At the back the wheels were hung on a fabricated steel rigid axle suspended on coil springs with concentric dampers. Lateral location was by a long Panhard rod, with a modified Watts linkage providing longitudinal location on both sides. These changes to the ideal Watts geometry caused the axle to twist

under suspension loads, which provided its own anti-roll action without the need for a separate anti-roll bar.

Once the car was announced, in November 1971, and it became clear how far the Alfasud had departed from established, and successful, Alfa practice, it was a matter for speculation about how the car's behaviour would live up to the standards of the marque. In retrospect, the most astonishing thing about the Alfasud was the way in which it lived up to, and in some cases exceeded, all these expectations.

It was clear that this was a very successful design indeed, and one that was at the very beginning of its development career. With a car weighing just 16.4cwt (830kg), or around 20 per cent less than the Spider 2000 two-seater, the power-

The engine installation of the Alfasud 1.2 TI. (LAT)

The standard Alfasud (left) and the more upmarket Alfasud L (right), the latter distinguishable by the bright horizontal bar across the grille. (Alfa Romeo archives)

to-weight ratio was better than that of the Giulietta TI. The top speed was 93mph (150kph), with a third-gear peak of 80mph (128kph). But the car's most powerful trump card, and its biggest surprise for the sceptics, was the brilliance of its handling.

When the Alfasud appeared on the British market in 1973, *Autocar* tested it and claimed that 'in all its dynamic respects the Alfasud sets new and even higher handling standards for front-drive cars'. Because of the

ingenious suspension geometry and the low roll rate, the magazine found none of the common interference between drive and steering mechanisms generally encountered with front-wheel drive cars, and went so far as to claim that 'the handling is better than on any other Alfa (which is saying a lot) and well ahead of all the other saloons in this very competitive class. In fact, we cannot think of a single saloon which takes corners with such contempt nor seems to hang on to the surfaces with such a leech-like grip.'

They were not alone. *Motor* praised cornering that was 'quite surprisingly neutral for a front-wheel-driven car with considerable front-weight bias'. Just about the only criticisms of the original design concerned the spacing of the ratios in the four-speed 'box, the off centre stiffening tunnel running along the floor of the passenger compartment, just like the transmission tunnel in a rear-drive car, which produced a cramped set of pedals on right-hand-drive cars, and some shortcomings in the standards of finish and build quality.

Although the car was (in almost all respects) a delight, the rest of the plan was soon causing concern. Demand soared, but output failed to keep pace. Alfa Romeo had originally received applications from 140,000 people who wanted to help make the car. They had interviewed 20,000 of these, and took on just half to get the project started. Initial output began at 70 cars a day, but this was planned to reach 500 cars a day after six months, with a full planned output of 1000 cars a day just a year after the launch.

It never happened. Absenteeism created one enormous problem, compounded by inadequate quality control, and this in a car where one of the main design priorities had been that it should be capable of being made by largely unskilled labour. Other failings were shared with the larger cars, and stemmed from the use of thinner steel for the body panels; this problem was intensified by a greater reliance on lower-cost recycled steel, where differences in the molecular structure

A new shape in the Alfasud line-up: the elegant little Alfasud Sprint coupé. This is the 1976 version. (Alfa Romeo archives)

The interior of the 1978 Alfasud 1.3-litre Super. (LAT)

made it more susceptible to corrosion, at a time when more road salt was being sprayed on the surface in winter, and acid rain was becoming a widespread environmental problem all over Europe.

Difficulties such as these threatened to cut off the car's potential in its prime. Already Alfa had planned a major development programme to make the most of the car's appeal and its performance potential. In November 1973 a TI version appeared, with a two-door body and some minor alterations to the engine, including a slight increase in the compression ratio to 9:1, and the replacement of the single carburettor by a double-choke unit; this raised the peak power output to 68bhp net (79bhp gross). Front and rear spoilers and quadruple headlamps were the main exterior changes, and other improvements included extra instruments mounted in the centre of the dash, a sporty

steering wheel with drilled spokes, and a five-speed gearbox to make better use of the increased power. Top speed climbed to 100mph (160kph) and the car's legendary handling now became part of an even more attractive package, which was forecast to sell in Britain for only £100 more than the basic saloon. It was actually priced at £1,717 on the road, roughly £300 more than the basic model.

The TI's launch coincided with the first anniversary of the introduction of the original Alfasud, by which time the plan had provided for a total of 175,000 of the basic saloon to have been made. The actual total was 78,000, ample proof of how far output had fallen behind schedule. Yet, to its credit, Alfa Romeo kept on developing the car to new heights of performance and appeal. In May 1974 the SE (Special Equipment) was introduced, to address some of the criticisms levelled at the basic model.

This had the four-door body, four-speed gearbox and the single-choke Solex carburettor of the original saloon, but with the higher compression ratio of the TI and a list of additional features including headrests on the front seats, a heated rear window, a cigar lighter and tachometer, and a laminated windscreen. This was all right as far as it went, but owners still complained, for example, about the lack of a bootlid prop, so that keeping the boot open while carrying heavy luggage meant lifting the lid right up to the point where it rested against the rear roofline, with consequent damage to the paintwork.

In January 1975 the Alfasud L appeared, taking the process a stage further with rubber-inset carpets on the floor, chromed bumper overriders, and a chrome strip along the door and window sills. However, there was little sign that the design's underlying faults were being corrected. For example, the offcentre position of the central reinforcement tunnel in the floor of the passenger compartment meant that the pedals on the right-hand-drive versions of the car were cramped too closely together. Anyone wearing anything other than the narrowest of shoes risked having to choose which pair of pedals they wanted to operate at once, clutch and brake, or brake and accelerator. Yet throughout the model's life, and that of its Sprint stablemate and successor, the fault was never eliminated.

Another persistent problem was the bonding of the windscreen to the body. For this to be successful, it was essential for the screen to be positioned very accurately indeed, and it was becoming increasingly clear that the locally-recruited workforce were having real problems doing this with sufficient consistency. One alternative was to revert to holding the screen in a rubber seal in the ordinary way, but this would mean that it ceased to take its share

Alfasud – the political background

To begin with, the Alfasud was smaller than the company's existing range, and of a completely different mechanical configuration. Then, it was to be made not in the Arese plant, or even its Portello predecessor, in the stronghold of the Northern Italian automobile industry, but in a new purpose-built plant at Pomigliano d'Arco near Naples, with a locally recruited workforce who would have to be trained in their new role as car assembly workers.

It was a radical and ambitious project. There was a certain logic behind it, but also a heavy risk. Although Alfa already owned the site – it had been a wartime aero-engine plant and was at the time making components for aero-engines and diesels – the Alfasud was to be turned out from an entirely new factory, the construction programme starting in 1968. Government grants were available for companies setting up in the South of Italy, to help alleviate chronic local unemployment, and Alfa's position as a State-backed company compelled it to take part in the project. It would involve a huge increase in output for an organisation long committed to the medium-scale production of specialist performance cars for reasonably upmarket customers.

The figures were daunting enough. Production would begin with a workforce of 5,000, with nine workers in every ten recruited from the Naples area. The eventual production target was 1000 cars a day, by which time the factory would employ 15,000 people. In other words, the little Alfasud would have to be sold at a price, and possess sufficient appeal, to attract upwards of 350,000 customers a year. Moreover, it would have to do this at a time when all the company's other models were selling at a combined rate of roughly a quarter of that figure.

This meant taking no chances at all with the engineering design of the car. To do the job on which everything else would depend, Alfa commissioned Rudolf Hruska, an Austrian engineer who had worked with Ferdinand Porsche before the war on the design of the Volkswagen Beetle and had helped develop the German 'Tiger' tank during the war; after the war he had again worked with Ferry Porsche on the Cisitalia racing car project to raise the funds to ransom Porsche Senior from a French prison, where he was being kept on charges of employing slave labour in wartime plants in France. He had worked for Alfa on the production of the 1900 and the Giulietta, and had then moved to Simca and Fiat before being lured back for the Alfasud project.

of the body stresses, and more redesign work would be needed.

After the effects of the Yom Kippur War of October 1973, and the resulting leap in oil prices, the Alfasud project underwent a radical change of direction. Up to that point the car had been conceived as a deliberate move away from the upmarket, sporting appeal of traditional Alfa Romeo models, and it was only the skill of the engineers and their belief in high levels of handling and a measure of performance that had led to the car being as popular as it was. After the oil crisis, and its crippling effect on sales of the established Alfa models, the status of the Alfasud changed

The 1982 Green Cloverleaf version of the Sprint. (LAT)

from a risky venture to a commercial lifebelt. If the company's survival depended on the Alfasud being repositioned as a sporty and comfortable prospect for the enthusiast driver, then that was exactly what would have to happen.

In the autumn of 1976 Alfa took the boldest step yet along this new road to prosperity with the introduction of the Alfasud Sprint, which used the same floorpan and running gear as the earlier saloons, but was fitted with a completely new Giugiaro coupé body that had no panels at all in common with the other cars. Its overall shape was a cross between his design for the VW Scirocco and the prototype he had recently shown for the Alfetta GT. In this case, the low overall height of the flat-four engine allowed an even lower bonnet line tapering down to a front end that

actually added 3 inches (7.5cm) to the car's overall length.

The coupé was 1 inch (25mm) wider than the Alfasud saloons, but a full 4 inches (10.0cm) lower. Although driver and passengers did well with leg and shoulder room, headroom was definitely meagre for taller occupants, especially in the rear seats. On the other hand, the elegant contours of the Sprint body made little difference to boot space. Not only did the boot have a reasonably wide semi-tailgate, but this was supported by two gas-filled struts to keep it hoisted well out of the way while loading or unloading.

Some compromises had to be made. The need to provide adequate stiffness at the rear of the car, with the larger bootlid, meant that the rear panel of the car had to remain fixed,

as part of the rear reinforcing box section, and luggage therefore had to be lifted in and out over it. The front end of the luggage 'box' also had to remain fixed, so it was impossible to make the most of the semi-hatchback structure and fit folding rear seats to turn the car into a semi-estate as well as a sports coupé.

Inside, the car had a new instrument panel, with the speedometer and tachometer in front of the driver and flanked by gauges for oil pressure and water temperature. The seats were in cloth, with carpets on the floor, and the generous window area made for a light and airy interior. All this opulence, together with the longer

'Performance has improved greatly – one is no longer a slave to the gear lever'

nose and the extra stiffening at the tail, increased the overall weight by 1.6cwt (80kg) over the saloons.

To give the Sprint the necessary performance to justify its name, an increase in engine size was clearly needed, and the chosen solution was to increase the stroke from 59mm to 64mm, which raised the capacity from 1186cc to 1286cc. With the carburettor, compression ratio and valve timing of the Alfasud TI, this produced 76bhp at 6,000rpm, enough to give the aerodynamically efficient Sprint a top speed of 102mph (163kph).

This engine added to the increasing complexities of the saloon range. In September 1976 the basic Alfasud saloon was given the option of a fifth gear ratio, in a variant called the Alfasud 5m, which took over from the Alfasud L. When fitted with the engine introduced on the Sprint, the

four-door 5m became the Alfasud 1300 Super, enjoying the power of the original TI, but with greater fuel economy.

This created another marketing problem, particularly in Britain. When the Sprint appeared in the UK in 1977 it cost £1000 more than the 1300 Super saloon, then priced at just under £3,000. For their extra money customers had a much better-looking car, but not enough additional performance to justify the jump in price. So the company increased the engine size by opening up the bores from 80mm to 84mm and lengthening the stroke all over again, from 64mm to 67.2mm, increasing the capacity from 1286cc to 1490cc. When fitted into the coupé, this produced the Sprint 1.5, with 85bhp at 5,800rpm, and a very slightly higher top speed of 105mph (168kph).

Motor Sport tested the 1.3 Sprint in November 1976, and said that 'one must add that the acceleration is not impressive unless you use the five-speed gearbox to the full'. On the other hand, *Motor* tried the 1300 TI a year later with the same engine and found that 'the larger engine more than justifies itself both in standing start acceleration and in its pull in the top two ratios, and also in its behaviour at lower revs'. When *Autosport* tested the Sprint 1.5, it commented that 'certainly the performance has improved out of all recognition. One is no longer a slave to the gear lever, and though its intelligent use ensures the best acceleration, the 1.5 will pick up from low speeds fairly briskly on the higher gears, when one is in no particular hurry.'

These additional engine options produced a whole raft of different models. An extra compromise was offered by combining the narrower bores of the original engines with the long stroke of the 1490cc version, to produce an intermediate engine of

1351cc. In the new Alfasud Super 1.3, fitted with the original carburation and compression ratio, it delivered 71bhp and a top speed of 93mph (149kph) in the Alfasud Super 1.3. Fitted in the two-door body to create the Alfasud TI 1.3, and given the TI's higher compression ratio and twin-choke Weber, it delivered 79bhp and gave a top speed of 98mph (157kph).

Using the 1490cc engine in the four-door and two-door bodies produced the Alfasud 1.5 Super, with 84bhp, and the Alfasud TI 1.5, with the same specification and power output (85bhp) as the Sprint 1.5 coupé. And below all these models in the range was the original 1186cc four-door saloon, now known simply as the Alfasud 1.2.

In some respects little had changed to the appearance of the cars, apart from the adoption of stripes running from the rearmost edge of the rear side window up to the rear edge of the roofline to identify model designations, and the availability of alloy wheels as optional extras. However, there were long overdue changes under the skin, as the company tried to get to grips at last with the perennial problems of corrosion.

This involved a detailed and far-reaching rustproofing programme, with heavier-quality underseal, phosphate coating, electrophoresis, and zinc-chrome treatment used under the body paint to give a longer-lasting finish. Panels that had shown themselves particularly susceptible to rust, such as the doors, bonnets, bootlids and, for some reason, fuel filler caps, were now to be made from steel that was pre-treated to build up a strongly rust-resistant zinc coating.

Zinc treatment was also specified for the frames around the openings for doors, bonnet and bootlid, as well as window surrounds and ventilation extraction grilles. Welded joints between panels were protected with

The 1.5-litre Sprint Trofeo from 1982. (LAT)

plastic sealant to prevent dust and moisture gathering in crevices, and confined spaces such as the body box sections were injected with polyurethane foam to prevent moisture build-up and resulting corrosion. Friction between metal parts and between trim components and the main bodyshell was prevented by fitting rubber stops, gaskets and buffers. Brightwork items such as bumpers, rain channels, handles and bootlid hinges, finally, were made from higher-specification stainless steel.

In 1980 the whole range was updated. The company called the new cars the Series III Alfasuds, although the designation was never used in any publicity material. Little

was done to change the basic shape of either version of the saloon, or of the Sprint. But subtle styling changes were all intended to aid the necessary move upmarket. The chrome bumpers were replaced by matt black protectors, which were wrapped right around the body as far as the wheelarches. The front bumper was reshaped to incorporate a revised chin spoiler, and protector strips were applied to the door sills, the sides of the doors where damage might result from careless parking, and the edges of the wheelarch openings.

Sportier wheels were fitted to all models in the range, and reshaped direction indicator clusters gave a new look to both the two-headlamp and four-headlamp versions of the car. The radiator shield was reshaped, smoothing out the two sharp top corners to make it look more like that fitted to Milan-built Alfas, and to

reinforce the car's identity as part of the company range. The grille was given more prominent horizontal bars, with a matt black finish. At the back the light clusters were now so large that half the lights were fitted on to the bootlid rather than the rear wing, and the whole process was underlined by a change in the rear-end model identification. Where this had previously read 'Alfasud 1.5', for example, it now read 'ALFA ROMEO Alfasud 1.5'.

At the same time, and for similar reasons, it was decided to offer increased engine power by the simple expedient of fitting twin double-choke carburettors and using a higher compression ratio on both the 1286cc and 1490cc engines fitted to the two different versions of the Sprint. With the compression ratio raised to 9.5:1 and the new twin-carburettor installation, the 1286cc engine delivered 86bhp, a whisker more than the original 1490cc engine, and sufficient to provide a top speed of 106mph (170kph) in what was now termed the Alfasud 1.3 Sprint Veloce. Oddly, Alfa must have felt that the Sprint's ancestry was clear enough anyway, since it dropped both 'Alfa Romeo' and 'Alfasud' from the rear boot script in favour of just 'Sprint Veloce 1.3'.

As usual with smaller-engined models of established Alfa favourites, the 1.3 was aimed mainly at customers who decided against the larger engine for reasons of taxation or economy, and only about one in ten Sprints were made with the smaller engine, none of them for sale in Britain. The 1490cc version, called the Alfasud 1.5 Sprint Veloce, now boasted 95bhp at 5,800rpm, and the top gear ratio was eased to provide more comfortable high-speed cruising, with a new top speed of 109mph (175kph) and acceleration sharp enough to see 60mph (96kph) on the speedometer in less than 11 seconds from a standing start.

The next step was to make this version of the engine available on the 1.5 TI saloon, which was now available in no fewer than three variations. Buyers could choose the single-carburettor TI with the old-style body, the twin-carburettor TI with some of the new modifications such as grille changes, bumpers and front and rear spoilers, and the full Veloce specification with twin carburettors and new styling. Those who opted for the Alfasud 1.5TI Veloce actually enjoyed acceleration that was slightly quicker than the Sprint equivalent, thanks to an appreciably lighter body, and a top speed of some 106mph (170kph), although the factory claimed that it was capable of 110mph (176kph).

If all this activity were not enough, the following year (1981) saw the introduction of a rear hatchback, made possible by stiffening the frame

Alfasuds in Britain

On the Italian market, buyers had a choice of 19 different model versions at the peak of the range's popularity in 1982. These varied from a basic four-seater, four-door saloon with a 63bhp 1.2-litre engine, right up to the 1.5-litre version of the Sprint coupé, delivering half as much power again. Because of the extra cost of producing right-hand-drive versions, British customers never had the choice of the full range. Their options began with the arrival of the basic model in August 1973, followed by the first of the TIs in March 1974. In June of that year the four-door SE (Special Equipment) version replaced the original saloon in UK dealerships. The SE was supposed to be replaced by the N (or Normale) and the more luxurious and expensive L versions in August 1975, but production problems held up supplies long enough to prolong the SE's availability in Britain until as late as March 1976.

In September 1976 the Alfasud N and L were in turn supposed to have been replaced by the 5m, but these too were in short supply because of difficulties at the factory, and only became generally available at the start of 1977. Other options at the time for British buyers included the two-door 68bhp TI, but from August the first of the longer-stroke 1300 TIs began to arrive, followed in October by the 68bhp, four-door 1300 Super. Even then, the earlier 1186cc TI and 5m were still available in the UK until May 1978.

From August 1978 the 1300 Super was replaced by the confusingly named 1.3 Super, which actually used the 1351cc engine in the four-door body. This engine was also used in the 1.3 TI, which appeared in Britain later that year, together with the 1490cc versions of the Super

saloon and the Sprint coupé, followed by the 1.5 TI in April 1979. By 1982 the UK Alfasud options had narrowed to the 1.5-litre Sprint, the 1.3-litre and 1.5-litre TIs, and the 1.3-litre and 1.5-litre saloons and hatchbacks.

One Alfasud that never made it to the UK at all was the Giardinetta, or estate car version, which appeared in June 1975. This used the front end of the two-door car with an estate body built up on the existing floorpan; it had a square-cut tail and a full opening tailgate. Because the engineers were able to build a stiffening box section right around the tailgate opening, this was the only version without the need for a rear sill. Almost 6,000 estates were made over seven years of production.

Other special versions never made it into production at all, such as the often rumoured but never seen Spider version of the Alfasud. On the other hand, individual specialists used the Alfasud as the basis for some interesting performance cars. In 1983, for example, UK Alfa dealers Bell & Colvill marketed a 1.5 TI fitted with a Garrett turbocharger to boost the power to 110bhp at 5,800rpm. The top speed rose to 120mph (192kph) and the car would reach 60mph in 9.1 seconds from a standing start. It sold for £5,995, appreciably less than the contemporary top-of-the-range Sprint.

around the larger opening panel as much as possible without making the rear pillars unacceptably thick, then trimming away metal from the rear box section to leave a U-shaped box with room for the rear seats to fold. The sides of the 'U' ran up the inner side of the wheelarch pressings, to connect with the roof arch, which now carried the recessed tailgate hinges. To add strength to the whole rear-end structure, a box section was added to each side of the body, running down from the top of the legs of the U-shaped box to another transverse reinforcement, which also formed the lower lip of the tailgate aperture.

This resulted in the only real compromise that the designers had to make with the ideal tailgate set-up. Because the transverse stiffening box under the lower tailgate lip had to be deep enough to do its job properly, it was still necessary to lift luggage in and out over a sill. On the other hand, the folding seats increased the total load space from 12cu ft (0.34cu m), which was a little less than the 14cu ft (0.39cu m) of the saloon, due to the extra internal stiffening structure, to a staggering 42cu ft (1.18cu m) with the seats folded flat. In addition, the rear boxes were used as storage spaces, with the right-hand one containing the jack and toolkit.

The new five-door Alfasuds were added to the range from the end of May 1982, when the different model options on existing body styles were also revised. The original 1.2-litre Alfasud kept the basic four-door body, while the Alfasud S (for Super) 1.2 had the five-door body, a 68bhp engine and the five-speed gearbox. One step up was provided by the Alfasud SC (for Super Comfort) 1.2, which had a more opulent interior.

The mid-range 1351cc engine was fitted to three-door and five-door bodies, but only in SC trim, and at the top of the hatchback range was

the *Quadrifoglio Oro*, or Gold Cloverleaf. This had the 1.5-litre engine in the 95bhp form used in the most powerful versions of the TI and the Sprint. It also had a long list of features ranging from cosmetic additions such as stainless-steel tailpipe extensions and contrasting upholstery to more practical revisions such as headlamp washers and wipers, and a wiper for the rear window.

The two-door TIs became three-door hatchbacks, and this slightly lighter body endowed them with fractionally more performance than those saloons with equivalent specifications. However, the traditional predominance of the TI version was restored in October 1982 with the introduction of the *Quadrifoglio Verde*, or Green Cloverleaf (based on the traditional emblem of the Alfa works racing team), which had new carburettor jets and revised induction pipework, modified cylinder heads and higher-lift camshafts, all this boosting the peak power of the twin-carburettor, 9.5:1 compression ratio, 1490cc engine from 95bhp to 105bhp at 5,800rpm. This raised the top speed to 112mph (180kph), while handling was improved by fitting low-profile tyres on new alloy wheels.

The body finish of the Green Cloverleaf was intended to set it apart from the rest of the range. The radiator was finished in Alfa red instead of chrome, a contrasting red and black band ran right around the body just above the door sills, and the car was only available in black, metallic grey or Alfa red. Meanwhile, in the spring of 1983, a similar prescription was applied to the Sprint, together with tighter suspension settings and a lower final-drive ratio. All the traditional chrome fittings were left black, except for the radiator shield, which, unlike that of the TI, was left with a bright finish, apart from on cars finished in black (other available colours were metallic light green or copper or silver, or

white or ivory or Alfa red), when the shield was finished in light green.

The comprehensive anti-rust treatment already outlined enabled the company to issue six-year anti-corrosion warranties, as final

The 1.7-litre Sprint is faster but rougher, raspier, and slightly crass in presentation

evidence that the early problems with runaway rust had been well and truly solved. Within the factory, output per man-shift had increased by 30 per cent over the difficult early days of the operation, and the whole range was selling well.

Yet this was the time when, in the final months of 1983, Alfa discontinued the saloon and TI ranges. The coupé continued to be sold as the Sprint for some time afterwards, latterly with a 1.7-litre engine, but the brilliant Alfasuds were replaced by the 33, a new range using the same engines, suspensions and floorpans to carry a completely new body. The 33 inherited some of the Sud's virtues, but in other areas proved disappointing.

Looking back at the popularity and influence of the Alfasud, it seems astonishing that the entire range was so varied, with almost 20 different model options at one stage, yet was still only in production for just 11 years. To the end of March 1984 the total output, including Sprints, amounted to just over a million, a respectable enough total by the company's existing standards, but a figure that should have been reached, under the original plan, after three years of production.

Beware the temptation to think that as Alfasuds became up-engined they lost the charm of the original. Yes, the first-of-line 1186cc saloons are sweet, delicate and ever so competent. But progressive improvements over the years were just that – progressive – with each ratcheting-up of cubic capacity and power bringing about a quantifiable bettering of the product.

The first Alfasuds are slow – 80mph (129kph) maximum, if conditions are against you – and lack low-down power. There is also no fifth gear, presumably as the modestly endowed flat-four would not cope. But you do have neutral cornering, superb adhesion and light and reaction-free steering, plus strong brakes and a supple ride. With good insulation from road noise and mechanical hubbub, the Sud is one

refined little motor car. It's just that you have to work it hard to deliver a decent performance.

As the car evolved, so it gained in flexibility (although no Sud is wonderfully flexible), while never losing that essential sweetness. And all the while that 'boxer' four-pot continued to deliver that rasping soundtrack that is so typically Alfasud. The 1300 models give a good dose of low-down muscle – pundits say it's the best of the bunch, at least in TI form – while the 1500 is demonstrably quicker, at the expense of some coarseness. In comparison, the 1.7-litre Sprint (a post-Sud Sud, if you like) seems to have lost the Sud charm: it's faster, but rougher, raspier

The Alfasud 1.5 TI *Quadrifoglio* from 1984. (LAT)

The end of the line, from austerity to luxury and performance – the interior of the 1989 1.7-litre Sprint *Quadrifoglio*. (LAT)

and ever so slightly crass in its presentation. A chrome-bumper 1.5 Sprint seems truer to what the car should be.

But whatever the motorisation, the Sud is an enthusiast's delight. You might find the gearchange a bit rubbery, but it is quick and precise, even if it lacks that feeling of metallic connection found in Giuliettas and Giulias. More important is that fabulous chassis. The absence of understeer is quite amazing, the Sud's neutrality being deeply impressive for an early-'70s design. Do what you want with the throttle: the car will hold its line. To exploit this tenacious and accurate roadholding is steering that is spot-on, being light, full of feel and quick – although not overmuch – in its responses. There's none of the lift-off tuck-in of the Mini generation of front-drivers, and you can drive the

Sud on brakes and steering – capitalising on the sharp well-weighted action of the all-disc set-up. Rounding out the picture, the ride is excellent, offering a perfect blend of control and comfort without any tendency to roll.

Truly this is a chassis of genius – although in 1.7-litre Sprint form the virtues are slightly debased, to the extent that the car is less neutral, heavier to steer, slightly knobbly in its ride, and prone to a degree of torque-steer. Too much power, and too much low-profile rubberware: that would seem to be the reason for the last coupé's lack of grace. Take your Alfasud pleasures more simply, lower down the range, and the experience will be more intense.

Buying Hints

1. Alfasuds suffer more from corrosion than any other Alfa, to the point where few early cars survive. In the worst instances a car can literally break in two. Not only this, but the metal on early cars is so poor that it is nearly impossible to weld in repair panels. The later cars are better protected from rust, but still demand extremely careful inspection.

2. The worst area for rust is across the front bulkhead, on which the steering rack mounts. Inspect closely under the heater box, master cylinder and battery.

3. Early Suds have the front screen bonded in place. This proved a constant source of trouble, with the screen coming unbonded and water getting underneath to cause rusting of the screen aperture and scuttle. Even later cars with rubber-mounted screens suffer from rust-blistering at the corner of the scuttle – and this is often worse than it at first appears.

4. The lower chassis rails are also liable to rot through, but the floorpan is generally fairly resistant to corrosion – except around the seat mountings. The sills, predictably, are also prone to rust, especially near the jacking points, and the front and rear valances may also have turned frilly.

5. The box section at the top of the inner front wing, where it meets the bulkhead, is another weak point: inspect the area around the battery and behind the washer bottle. Although the front strut mountings tend to stay sound, the inner wing close to the struts can rust badly.

6. The longer doors on two-door models put a strain on the flimsy hinges and on the 'A' pillar. Gradually the pillar will crumble under the strain, while the action of the sagging door hitting the 'B' post will lead to corrosion here.

7. The rear screen on early cars was, like the windscreen, bonded in place; again this came unstuck to cause leaks, resulting in corrosion around the aperture and allowing water into the boot to rot it out. On hatchbacks, water lies at the bottom corners of the rear screen, causing rust in the adjacent metalwork. Adding to the fun, boot hinges on first-generation cars seize easily, then snap, while related distortion of the bootlid could have let water into the boot.

8. The lower wishbones can themselves rot, while at the rear the beam axle can corrode where the spring sits on the beam; inspect the bottom of the beam carefully.

9. The rear disc brakes do little work, and can seize. At the front, leaks from the front callipers are common.

10. Engines are strong, and last well so long as cam-belt changes take place at the recommended 36,000-mile intervals. A clattering betrays wear in the cam lobes on later cars with the 1500cc engine; these later examples also suffer from head-gasket problems. Not surprisingly, if an engine has been over-revved the big ends can suffer. The belt tensioner is another point to check: with the engine running, it should spin smoothly with no evidence of wobbly free play. A sluggish and noisy tensioner needs attention.

11. Gearboxes last well, with the main weakness being fading synchromesh on second gear. In addition, the bushes in the gear linkage wear rapidly, leading to sloppiness and difficult gear selection, but this is cheap to fix.

12. The universal joints are more robust than normal, but check all the same for wear by listening for clicking while accelerating at low speed on full lock.

Alfetta Saloons *and GTs*

The original Alfetta, introduced in 1972, was fitted with the same twin-cam 'four' as used in the 1750 range, although this was now described as a 1.8-litre engine. (Alfa Romeo archives)

By the 1970s the original and brilliantly successful inspiration that had produced the 1900s, the Giuliettas, the Giulias, the 1750s and ultimately the 2000s, was beginning to show signs of age and obsolescence at last. What was clearly needed, if Alfa was to be able to maintain its image for sound, advanced engineering and high-performance cars, was a way of reversing the trend towards nose-heaviness that had intensified with the later models, as well as a means of providing independent rear suspension to allow the company's production cars to re-establish their ascendancy in handling and roadholding over their closest competitors.

This was a radical enough change after almost a quarter of a century with the original system, but more

was to come. Alfa was also concerned about the distribution of the main masses within the car's structure, and sports-racing car design had already proved beyond reasonable doubt that the way to provide first-class handling was to concentrate the weight of the engine, gearbox and final drive as close to the car's centre of gravity as possible. Unfortunately, this would have meant turning the priorities of a production car inside out, and locating all the major mechanical assemblies in the middle of the car, displacing the passenger compartment.

Instead the company opted for the next best thing, which was to place the major mechanical assemblies at

Could the pedigree of the best racing Alfas help solve the problems of production cars?

opposite ends of the car, as close as possible to the wheel centres, but with the total weight more evenly divided between front and rear. Together with de Dion rear suspension, this had been the solution adopted in the splendid Alfetta Grand Prix cars, which had won the company two post-war GP World Championships in one of the most glorious chapters of Alfa Romeo history. Could the pedigree of the most successful of racing Alfas be used to solve the problems of a production model 20 years later, in a unique demonstration of competition belatedly improving the breed?

The GP set-up had involved placing the clutch and gearbox next to the differential at the back of the car. The intention for the production car was to mount all these assemblies in a single light-alloy casing together with inboard rear disc brakes, and to fix it

Alfetta 1.8 and 1.6
1972–1984

ENGINE:
Four-cylinder, twin ohc

Bore x stroke	80 x 88.5mm (1.8)
	78 x 82mm (1.6)
Capacity	1779cc (1.8)
	1570cc (1.6)
Power	122bhp (1.8)
	108bhp (1.6)

TRANSMISSION:
Five-speed gearbox

Final drive	4.100:1

BODY STYLE:
Four-door saloon

PERFORMANCE:
(from contemporary sources)

Max speed	110mph (176kph)
0–60mph (97kph)	10.7 seconds

LENGTH:	14ft 3in (4.28m)
WIDTH:	5ft 6in (1.62m)
WHEELBASE:	8ft 4in (2.51m)

Alfetta 2000
1977–84

As Alfetta 1.8 except:

Bore x stroke	84 x 88.5mm
Capacity	1962cc
Power	140bhp

PERFORMANCE:
(from contemporary sources)

Max speed	113mph (181kph)
0–60mph (97kph)	9.4 seconds

Alfetta GT
1974–76

As Alfetta 1.8 except:
BODY STYLE: Four-seater coupé

LENGTH:	14ft 3in (4.19m)
WIDTH:	5ft 6in (1.67m)
WHEELBASE:	7ft 10.5in (2.40m)

Alfetta 2000 GTV
1976–86

As Alfetta GT except:

Bore x stroke	84 x 88.5mm
Capacity	1962cc
Power	130bhp

PERFORMANCE:
(from contemporary sources)

Max speed	120mph (205kph)
0–60mph (97kph)	9.4 seconds

Giulietta 1.6

As Alfetta 1.6 except:
PERFORMANCE:
(from contemporary sources)

Max speed	106mph (170kph)
0–60mph (97kph)	12.2 seconds

LENGTH:	13ft 9.8in (4.21m)
WIDTH:	5ft 5in (1.65m)
WHEELBASE:	8ft 2.8in (2.51m)

Alfa GTV6
1981–86

As Alfetta GTV except:
ENGINE:
V6, single ohc per bank

Bore x stroke	88 x 68.3mm
Capacity	2492cc
Power	160bhp
Max speed	128mph (205kph)
0–60mph (97kph)	8.9 seconds

NUMBER BUILT:

Alfetta Berlina	475,743
1.6 GTV	16,923
1.8/2000 GTV	96,969
GTV6	22,380

The interior of the Alfetta – a 1.6, in this instance – shows how far luxury had come from the days of the original 1900 and Giulietta models. (Alfa Romeo archives)

to the body structure so that it added nothing to the unsprung weight. This would produce almost perfectly even weight distribution between the front and rear wheels, and the reduced load on the front suspension would also allow a revision of the steering geometry to lighten steering effort. In addition, the front suspension was switched to double wishbones and longitudinal torsion bars, tuned to respond in a way that would reduce at long last the familiar Alfa body roll on the entry to corners.

Engineering improvements rarely come without a price-tag attached, and in this case there were formidable development problems in making an arrangement that had worked well under racing conditions acceptable for a production car. One inherent problem was the propshaft, which was now turning at crankshaft speed instead of at the gearbox output speed. This caused terrible

problems with vibration and resonances, all of which had to be carefully tuned out of the system, aided by a two-piece propshaft linked by rubber couplings.

The second problem was the position of the gearbox, which would no longer allow the direct linkage that had been such an attractive feature in a succession of models. Instead, the gear lever was linked to the box through a potentially troublesome succession of cables, rods and linkages, which were to prove a persistent problem throughout the life of the model; even when the system worked well, it lacked the precision of the old one.

The first production model appeared in May 1972, and given the origins of its basic design it provided Alfa with an even better opportunity to trade on past glories than had the 1750. It revived the name of Alfetta, but instead of a GP single-seater, the name was now applied to a saloon. Very slightly shorter and wider than the 2000 Berlina, the Alfetta, which was Satta's last design, had a neat combination of slab sides and sharp edges that lent it a distinctly crisp and sporty character, compared with the Giulia and its successors. Careful wind-tunnel testing produced an efficient aerodynamic profile that was very slightly wedge-shaped, with a low bonnet line sweeping back to end in a high tail that also provided a large boot.

Inside, the car provided room for five people in deeply upholstered seats covered in soft fabric. The steering column was adjustable for height, and a matching speedometer and tachometer were set in a binnacle behind the steering wheel, with three smaller dials in between them to monitor fuel tank contents, water temperature and time of day. An oil pressure gauge was set into the tachometer dial, and the car was provided with a whole range of small storage spaces, from a dashboard glovebox to a small parcel tray, a small space in the centre console and map pockets in the backs of the two front seats.

Strangely, Alfa did not choose the largest version of the classic twin-cam 'four' to power the new car, at least at first. Instead, the 1779cc version found in the recently replaced 1750 was used, although to avoid mixing the historical allusions the model was identified as the Alfetta 1.8. The only change was an increase in the compression ratio from 9:1 to 9.5:1, which lifted the power peak slightly from 118bhp to 122bhp at the same speed of 5,500rpm. Although the car was virtually identical in weight to the 1750 Berlina, the increase in power produced no increase in top speed, which remained at 112mph (180kph).

Sadly, the car's debut was to be a less than happy one. By the time of its appearance industrial unrest had

Alfetta – inspiration for a new rear suspension

Many of the earlier independent rear suspensions had relied on swing axles, which, under certain conditions, could produce a sudden and usually terminal transition from understeer to dramatic oversteer. This was partly why the large and stupendously powerful pre-war Auto-Union Grand Prix cars had been fearsomely difficult to drive, and the only reason why later Mercedes swing-axle rear suspension systems had not suffered from the same problems was their ingenious low-pivot geometry, which avoided any tendency towards sudden camber changes.

Alfa decided to avoid this problem – and the lesser failings of semi-trailing independent rear ends – by using a de Dion rear axle. This works by linking both rear wheels with a tube to keep them upright and in line so that camber changes are impossible. Because the unsprung weight of the whole system is reduced to that of the tube alone, the suspension is able to respond well to bumps and changes in road surface camber without large amounts of axle hop or tramp.

As before, Alfa's engineers were determined that the whole set-up would be located as precisely as possible. To ensure this, they provided longitudinal struts to connect the suspension to a body crossmember, and an anti-roll bar. In addition they used a Watts linkage with the centre of the parallelogram fixed to the middle of the de Dion tube, and the outer ends of the two bars fitted to the suspension pivots, so as to eliminate any unwanted sideways play in the system.

spread to Milan, and it was to be a year before the Alfetta entered full production. When it did, its prospects were marred by persistent reports of the near impossibility of engaging first gear, coupled with the usual complaints about the imbalance between the location of the pedals and the steering wheel for taller drivers, and some hints that the handling was less than perfect.

Autosport tested the car at its Trieste launch, and gave it praise indeed. 'The car is beautifully balanced, light to handle, and gives plenty of messages through the steering,' wrote the magazine. 'Alfa Romeos have always cornered well, but this one excels its predecessors in the way it sticks to the road when flung through bumpy curves. . . One can use full throttle on the lower gears on grease and mud, because the de Dion axle does its job and the weight distribution is right.' About the only

The original instrument layout for the Alfetta GT had the rev-counter set in front of the driver with the speedometer banished to the centre panel along with the subsidiary instruments; this arrangement was later reversed. (Alfa Romeo archives)

criticisms made of a presumably well set-up test car were a lack of bite in the brakes for emergencies, and a first gear that tended to 'balk on occasion when engaged from rest'.

Others were less happy about the car's accomplishments. *Motor Sport* tried one in the UK two years after the original launch, and complained of an insensitive throttle pedal that had not been obvious on the left-hand-drive launch cars. It went on to claim that wheelspin was easily provoked under hard acceleration out of tight, damp corners or bumpy, dry corners. In some cases the magazine reported strong understeer, and in others equally strong oversteer, although it also found that correction of tail-end breakaway was extremely easy, but speculated that part of the problem might lie with the tyres fitted to the test car.

Motor Sport found that the gear ratios 'proved an absolute delight, all five arranged in a manner which encouraged their constant use'. However, the gearchange was 'notchy when cold, 1st gear was often difficult to engage from rest, and 2nd gear synchromesh could be beaten easily. But once warm, the five speeds . . . could be engaged rapidly and accurately via the long, rearwards-pointing remote control.' Perhaps the testers were close to the truth when they concluded that expectations had been raised too high because of the car's unusual design and the company's own publicity, but that on price and performance it still beat most of its competitors 'into a cocked hat'.

In fact, all Alfa's work on associating the car with its racing past (which *Road Test* claimed had been the sole reason for all the complexity) was largely wasted in the American market. *Motor Trend* summed it up by saying that 'there is nothing deader than a dead racing car, and when that retirement has been on for a quarter of a century, dead is very dead indeed.' After the initial publicity drive, a compromise was agreed: in Europe the car would remain the Alfetta, but in the US it would be marketed simply as the Alfa Romeo Sports Sedan, which rather lost the point of the changes.

The second model in the new range was shown to the press in June 1974.

This was the Alfetta GT, a four-seat coupé designed originally by Giugiaro but subsequently modified by Alfa's styling department in the light of wind-tunnel testing. According to Alfa, this produced a commendably low drag coefficient of 0.39, but according to *Road Test* it so distorted Giugiaro's original concept that he refused to have anything more to do with the project. Whatever the truth of the matter, the GT looked very different from its stablemate, with a wheelbase shortened by almost 4½ inches. The car was 2¼ inches (9cm) shorter, 1.7 inches (4cm) wider, and 4 inches (10cm) lower than the

The Alfetta 1.6 was introduced in 1975, with a single pair of headlamps to distinguish it from its 1.8-litre parent. (Alfa Romeo archives)

The 2-litre version of the Alfetta GT was identified as the Alfetta Gran Turismo Veloce (or GTV). The letters 'GTV' cut out in the rear extractor panels proved very difficult to keep clean. (LAT)

its mind and exchanged the two main instruments.

There were two more peculiarities. Although it was slightly smaller than the saloon, the GT was only 22lb (10kg) lighter, and the engine tune and power output were exactly the same, as was the top speed of 112mph (180kph). Clearly, UK customers were to be persuaded to spend £3,797, compared with around £2,300 for the saloon, purely for the GT's looks and sporting image, rather than because of any performance advantage.

When the press got to grips with the GT, there were criticisms regarding the range of adjustment available for the driver (once again, a case of pedals too near, wheel too far) and difficulties with the gearchange. It was already clear that the gearchange problems were a matter of individual adjustment and seemed to vary very much from car to car. Perhaps more significant from Alfa's point of view were the assessments of the car's handling. This was supposed to be the primary reason for all the mechanical complexity, yet there were few of the superlatives that the Giuliettas and the Giulias used to attract.

Over the years, however, the model sold tolerably well, and Alfa Romeo widened the range by introducing two other engines. First was the Giulia 1570cc engine, now with a 9.5:1 compression ratio (but 9:1 for the GT, oddly) and fitted with twin double-choke carburettors, delivering 108bhp in the saloon and 109bhp in the GT. This was introduced in 1975 for the saloon, which in this form was identified by a single pair of headlamps and a single bright horizontal strip on the front end of the car. The top speed dropped slightly to 110mph (176kph), as did that of the revised 1.8-litre version at the time.

In 1976 the 1.8 Alfetta GT was replaced by two versions, one fitted with the 1570cc engine and named the Alfetta GT 1.6, and the other with

saloon, and owed very little in styling terms to any previous Alfa Romeo.

The mechanical set-up, suspension and running gear were all identical to those of the saloon. The difference was in the body shape, which incorporated a more discernible wedge from a low nose, through a steeply raked windscreen, to a high tail ending in a sharp rear cut-off. The rear panel, including the rear window and the bootlid, opened as a single hatch, although the usefulness of this was limited by the high rear sill and the fact that the rear seats were not made to fold. An ingenious linkage slid the front seats forward as the backs were folded, to improve access to the reasonably roomy rear compartment.

The most unusual feature of the interior was the instrumentation. Bowing to its association with Alfa's Championship-winning GP car, the only instrument located in the driver's sightline was a tachometer. The speedometer was set, with the subsidiary instruments, in a binnacle mounted in the centre of the dashboard, where it was less than easy to view at a glance. Eventually, after a whole series of road tests complained bitterly about the stupidity of the arrangement for road driving, Alfa Romeo changed the bigger-valved 1962cc unit used by the 2000 series of models, this being officially named the GTV 2000. Both were given the 9:1 compression ratio and a pair of double-choke carburettors; peak power outputs were 109 and 130bhp respectively.

Top speed remained 112mph (180kph) for the 1.6-litre version, but rose to just over 120mph for the larger 2-litre car, thanks to both versions having identical weights of 19.7cwt (1000kg). The GTV was additionally distinguished by replacing the louvred air extraction vent on the rear quarters by a stylised 'GTV' logo, which had sharp edges and was almost impossible to clean.

Encouragingly for the company, the press thought both cars a great

improvement. Two magazines renowned for not pulling their punches gave an unequivocal thumbs-up to both extremes of the new model ranges. Trying an Alfetta 1.6 saloon in Italy, *Car* observed that 'there is noticeably less punch in fourth and fifth, making overtaking take longer, but the drop in power is not hard to live with.' In terms of handling, it wrote, 'the 1.6 doesn't have quite enough under the bonnet to overcome the tremendous grip of the de Dion rear suspension, so oversteer is less likely.' Overall, 'the 1.6 has all the sweetness – indeed, sheer brilliance – of the normal Alfetta,' concluded the magazine.

For *Motor Sport* the GTV 2000 was 'beautiful, comfortable, quiet – and expensive, but worth it'. It found the

From the front, the Alfetta GTV looked squat, sleek and powerful. (LAT)

The top-of-the-range Alfetta 2000 saloon was identified by a single pair of rectangular headlamps. Contemporary publicity stressed the model's 'jet-set' associations. (Alfa Romeo archives)

handling. In all, it found the Alfa 'a car of superb balance, obviously greatly benefiting from its weight distribution'. The car's quietness, in terms of road noise, mechanical noise and wind noise also came in for real praise, as did the 'magnificent traction' and brakes 'which cannot be too highly praised'. Overall it classed the GTV as 'a nimble thoroughbred' with a responsive and flexible engine and gear ratios that were well spaced for brisk performance, even if they were not that easy to select!

When I sampled the original 1.8-litre Alfetta my initial reaction was one of disappointment. The car seemed slower than the 1750 saloon, partly through the extra weight it carried, but also as a result of the vague gearchange. Every change of ratio was an unpredictable business, slowing down driving and diluting any pleasure to be obtained from the undoubtedly high standards of chassis behaviour – the latter marred only by steering on the heavy and low-geared side. Fortunately a 2000 Berlina seemed much improved, with a zippier performance and a better-honed gearchange – although the latter did vary a lot from car to car.

Confirmation that the new Alfa mechanical configuration could work came with a GTV: the gearshift was reasonably precise – although still way short of the crispness of that of a front-gearbox Alfa – and cross-country performance and handling compared well with that of contemporary rivals. One frightening emergency on black ice certainly proved the worth of the Alfetta's perfect front-to-rear weight balance.

seating position was 'satisfactory – for the first time in an Alfetta', and reported that second gear was 'horribly difficult to engage when the 'box is cold'. In fact, the writer found the change both notchy and baulky, especially into first and second 'into which cogs the test car sometimes needed an extraordinary amount of force', a failing 'out of keeping with the thoroughbred spirit of the rest of the running gear'.

On the other hand, *Motor Sport* was delighted with the lightness and precision of the steering, the comfort of the ride and the excellence of the

In 1975 a 2-litre version of the Alfetta saloon was introduced in the US, again with fuel injection instead of carburettors. Two years later, in February 1977, the European model range was completed by the announcement of the Alfetta 2000, with a 9:1 compression ratio, a pair of double-choke carburettors, and a power output of 140bhp, giving a top speed of more than 115mph (185kph).

The interior was revised to provide greater comfort and an improved layout of controls and instruments, while on the outside the chief changes were the replacement of the circular headlamps used in the smaller-engined cars by a single pair of rectangular lamps, and the fitting of deeper front bumpers incorporating the indicators. *Autosport* tested the 2000 in April 1978 and hailed it as 'a brilliant design which makes many of its competitors seem dull and old-fashioned'. Despite the earlier complaints, it seemed as if Alfa Romeo had finally struck gold with this latest and most unconventional range of models.

Sadly for Alfa's hopes, however, the Alfetta never really did well in commercial terms. By 1984 it was a much better car in its final 2.0 Gold

Alfetta – a different perspective, or not?

A contrary viewpoint was put forward by *Road Test* in a design analysis of the car, when the magazine set out to prove that Alfa had got its initial priorities wrong, and had then compounded the problem by setting out to attain them in the worst way possible. In a comprehensive hatchet job, the writer claimed that too much money and attention had been paid to dubious engineering changes for insufficient reason. The de Dion rear suspension was discredited as being no better, although a lot more expensive, than the old, properly located rigid axle system. The torsion bar front suspension was said to be heavier, more expensive and more difficult to engineer with a variable rate than coil springs would have been. And the engine-

transmission split was said to be a 'mechanic's nightmare, for to change the clutch disc it is probably necessary to remove the unit from the vehicle'.

However, even *Road Test* seemed to change its mind with the passing of time. When it tested the GTV in December 1977, it called it 'a solid, pretty little car that's great fun to drive'. In spite of the earlier criticisms, the magazine was now able to say 'Sit in an Alfa, in any of the new models. That five-speed transmission, the look and feel of the controls, the pleasant rasp of the venerable Alfa double overhead-cam four – it all can mean only one thing: here's a car designed to be driven.' Acceptance, it seemed, had finally come at last.

The final Alfetta was the *Quadrifoglio d'Oro* ('Gold Cloverleaf') version of the Alfetta 2000, with quadruple headlamps, foglamps, extra chrome, deeper energy-absorbing bumpers, and much-needed better anti-corrosion protection. (LAT)

By 1979 the Giulietta was available in 1.3-litre, 1.6-litre and 1.8-litre versions, and a year later the line-up was completed with a 2-litre Giulietta. (LAT)

Cloverleaf form, with fuel injection, electronic ignition and two-position inlet valve timing ('Variable Valve Timing') to provide smaller overlap for starting and flexibility at low speeds, together with standard settings for high-speed running. Unfortunately, an increase in power and torque was largely wasted by a change in the final drive ratio that actually had the effect of making the driver use the gearbox more rather than less often. Given the appalling problems with the long linkages between lever and 'box, this was a well-aimed shot in the foot for the car's sales appeal.

Nine months after the unveiling of the Alfetta 2000, a new model appeared with the same mechanicals in a fresh and slightly smaller body. This continued the names-from-the-past theme, but with a much more recent

ancestor in mind. The new Giulietta featured a neat, wedge-shaped body with squared-off contours that lent it a passing family resemblance to the Alfetta saloon.

This Giulietta used the larger-bore, shorter-stroke 80mm by 67.5mm, 1357cc twin-cam developed originally for the GTA, turning out 95bhp at 6,000rpm. The larger model was fitted with the 1570cc Giulia engine in 109bhp Alfetta GT 1.6 form. The car was, at 20cwt (1,020kg), a significant 1.4cwt (70kg) lighter than the Alfetta 2000, and the top speeds were 103mph (165kph) for the Giulietta 1.3, and 109mph (175kph) for the Giulietta 1.6. Later, the 1.8-litre engine was offered in a Giulietta, and to complete the line-up 1980 saw the addition of a 115mph (185kph) 1962cc variant.

Buying Hints

1. The body quality on early Alfettas was poor; but later cars are better, as is the Giulietta, which from the start had better rustproofing and made extensive use of zinc-coated steel. Inner and outer wings, sills and door bottoms are all prone to rot on the Alfetta and its sister GTV models. Sill trims on body-kitted cars may make matters worse by trapping dirt and moisture.

2. A particular weak point is towards the bottom of the inner wings, where the front crossmember runs across the car. Additionally the splashguards at the front and rear of the inner wings are notorious for harbouring road dirt. The boot floor and spare wheel well may also suffer from rust, with the GTV6 prone to corrosion of the battery box inside the boot.

3. Early Alfettas and GTVs suffer from water being trapped behind the screen rubbers, especially if the drain holes have become blocked. Also attracting rust are the quarterlight and (on the GTV) the side-window guides.

4. The gearshift is frequently sloppy and imprecise, and the gearbox is likely to have suffered from insensitive handling and use of an incorrect type of oil. Re-bushing and careful adjustment by an expert will considerably improve things, and a high-quality synthetic oil such as Agip 75/90 can transform the shift quality. Later Isostatic linkages are more complex, and supposedly more accurate, but a properly set-up early shift should be perfectly satisfactory. The change is not fast, and should not be rushed, especially before the oil is fully warm: impatience of this variety is the reason why second-gear synchromesh is often poor.

5. The differential can leak oil through the side seals, while the rear wheel bearings frequently suffer from excess wear. A further rear-end malady often encountered is disintegration of the gearbox mountings on the clutch cover. This is betrayed by thumps from the rear when pulling away. Driveline harshness can also be a result of the rubber doughnut couplings in the propshaft starting to fail, or the centre bearing suffering from wear. Inspection of the car on a garage ramp should confirm these points.

6. The dampers are notoriously weak on Alfettas and Giuliettas, and can usefully be replaced by adjustable Spaxes or similar. Carry out the usual 'bounce' test to see how much life there is in the shocks. At the rear, the spring pans on the de Dion axle corrode badly.

7. Uneven front tyre wear may be a result of incorrect camber: this can be adjusted.

8. A rough tickover can aggravate other drivetrain failings: poor adjustment of the carbs is all too common.

9. The brakes should be excellent, but fitting and adjustment of the rear pads is often carried out incorrectly; worse, lubrication of the handbrake mechanism is frequently neglected. A poor handbrake or one with excessive travel is likely to indicate that the self-adjusting mechanism has not been set up correctly, as is over-long pedal travel.

10. Early V6 engines can suffer from valve guide wear, and there are also problems with the guide oil seals; check for blue smoke on the over-run. Check also for oil leaks from the hydraulic timing-belt tensioners: if this is really bad it could cause the belt to slip or snap, with nastily expensive consequences.

11. All the Alfetta series of Alfa Romeos demand sensitive attention. A good service history – not necessarily from an Alfa dealer but certainly from a well-regarded specialist – is the ideal for which to aim.

Alfas of the
1980s & '90s

A direct descendant of the Alfasud and made in the same factory, the Alfa 33 had a strong family resemblance to the new Giuliettas. (Alfa Romeo archives)

Although in some respects Alfa Romeo had done astonishingly well in steering a successful course through the minefield of the post-war automobile market, which during more than three decades of intensifying competition had seen many cherished names disappear in close-downs or take-overs, the company's time was fast running out. Government backing for almost half a century had kept harsh commercial realities at arm's length, but there are limits to the depths of even institutional pockets. By the start of the 1980s some progress had been made with solving the worst problems of build quality and corrosion resistance. Unfortunately, convincing the buying public would be a much more difficult task, at a time when the company's traditional engineering inspiration was showing signs of running out.

The Alfasud range had done wonders in commercial terms, even if it had never quite fulfilled Alfa's ambitions.

When the range had been discontinued (apart from the Sprint) in late 1983, the market had changed out of all recognition since the start of the project. The moving of the Sud range upmarket had increased the return on each car and had eventually solved the problem of its inability to meet the initial customer demand. Its successor would never need to be made in the same enormous numbers, which would leave some factory capacity free for something else altogether.

The car that replaced the Alfasud was yet another to follow the trend of naming new models to make the most of the company's sporting and racing heritage. In this case, as with the new Giulietta, it used a name from the very recent past. The Alfa rear-engined Tipo 33 Sports Prototype had been introduced in 1967, and just over a decade and a half later the Alfa 33 road car made its appearance. This used the same floorpan, engines, transmissions and suspensions as the Alfasuds, but with a new shell having lines more in keeping with the contemporary Giulietta.

The rest of the factory capacity at Pomigliano d'Arco was to be used to produce an entirely new mass-market Alfa. This was a new collaborative venture between Alfa Romeo and the giant Japanese producer Nissan, and

Unfortunately the badge was about the only positive aspect of the Arna

involved building a version of the Nissan Cherry, fitted with some Alfasud and 33 components, and badged as the Alfa Romeo Arna (for Alfa Romeo Nissan Auto). Unfortunately, the badge was just about the only positive aspect of a car that seemed to have been conceived with the deliberate aim of

eliminating everything which had made Alfas stand out from their competitors, in terms of their style and individuality. Nissan customers could see no reason for paying more for a car with other people's components, while traditional Alfa buyers were even less inclined to order a car that looked like any other Nissan Cherry, even though the mechanicals were different. The projected annual production for the car was 60,000 vehicles, but over three years the company produced rather less than that. It was the Alfasud story all over again.

Fortunately for Alfa Romeo, the 33 series did rather better. The car was built on a new production line, with a higher proportion of robot assembly technology, and proper attention being paid from the beginning to rustproofing and quality control. However, there was initial criticism about its disappointing performance and handling. In fact, the car's

The Alfa 6 was launched as a contender in the company's battle against BMW. The body style was a reworking of the basic Alfetta shape. (Alfa Romeo archives)

The fitting of the six-cylinder engine to the Alfetta GTV produced the Alfa GTV6, distinguishable by the cut-out in the top of the bonnet. (LAT)

The V6 engine fitted tightly under the GTV6 bonnet. (LAT)

acceleration and top speed compared well with even the later Alfasuds, and if the ride was softer and the tendency to roll more in

keeping with Alfa's past, there was no doubt that the different versions of the 33, which included an estate car and a four-wheel-drive version (even on the UK market) did hold the road reasonably well. Unfortunately, time and the market had moved on, and they lacked the sheer exuberant appeal of their smaller and more agile predecessors, and sales began an ominous fall.

Back in Milan, Alfa was having to rely on its Alfettas and Giuliettas to maintain its share of the traditional market sectors. In 1979 a new model was introduced to extend its range further upmarket. This was the Alfa 6, the first six-cylinder Alfa since the demise of the 2600 series more than a decade before, and it was powered by a new 'over-square' V6 engine of 2492cc, fitted with no fewer than six Dellorto carburettors and delivering 160bhp at 6,000rpm. This unit was fitted into an adapted Alfetta body, but with an orthodox gearbox rather than the rear-mounted set-up that on the Alfetta had so disappointed legions of testers and owners alike.

Although the top speed was a brisk 122mph (195kph), the car failed to match Alfa's hopes from the beginning. The styling was criticised as dated and the engine as rough and unresponsive, while the ZF sourced 5-speed gearbox, with its dog's leg first, was not universally liked. Significantly, for the UK market the 6 was only available as an automatic, which, whatever its other virtues in avoiding the need to wrestle with an uncooperative manual lever, seemed to cut right across the priorities that had made customers want to buy Alfas in the past. The combination was unlikely to solve Alfa's problems.

At the beginning of 1981 the same engine was offered in a top-of-the-range Alfetta GT coupé, marketed as the GTV6. This used a fuel-injection version of the V6 engine, with identical power and torque, but the result was a transformation. *Car* had tried the Alfa 6 saloon and been bitterly disappointed, placing the car last in a three-model comparison test. When it tested the GTV6, it reported happily that the 'gorgeous engine complements the outfit like you'd never believe, after reading those reports on the saloon'.

The Australian journal *Wheels* explained that 'the experts were sceptical because it was *that* engine.

The engine had been transformed and the GTV6 got rave reviews

The one fitted to the Alfa 6 sedan, that most un-Alfa of Alfas, which has generally been panned. The sceptics were wrong. The V6 might have been a temperamental mistress for the

Alfa 33
1983–1994

ENGINE:
Front longitudinal boxer four-cylinder – capacities ranging from 1186cc to 1712cc or three-cylinder in-line 1779cc turbo diesel. *Power output:* from 68bhp to 107bhp (petrol); 72bhp (turbo diesel)

TRANSMISSION:
Five-speed gearbox

BODY STYLE:
Four door saloon or five-door Sportwagon estate

PERFORMANCE:
Top speed: from 100mph (162kph) to 130mph (207kph)

Alfa 75
1985–1992

ENGINE:
Front longitudinal four-cylinder – capacities ranging from 1570cc to 1962cc or four-cylinder in-line 1995cc turbo diesel or six-cylinder 60-degree V6 of either 2492cc or 2959cc. *Power output:* from 110bhp to 148bhp (four-cylinder petrol engines); 95bhp (turbo diesel); 156bhp to 188bhp (V6 petrol engines)

TRANSMISSION:
Five-speed gearbox

BODY STYLE:
Four door saloon

PERFORMANCE:
Top speed: from 109mph (175kph) to 137mph (220kph)

Alfa 155
1992–1998

ENGINE:
Front transverse four-cylinder in-line engine – capacities ranging from 1773cc to 1970cc or four-cylinder in-line 1929cc or 2499cc turbo diesel or six-cylinder 60 degree V6 (2492cc). *Power output:* from 126bhp to 186bhp (petrol); 90bhp to 125bhp (turbo diesel); 165bhp (V6 petrol engine)

TRANSMISSION:
Five-speed gearbox

BODY STYLE:
Four door saloon

PERFORMANCE:
Top speed: from 112mph (180kph) to 141mph (225kph)

Alfa 145/146
Series 1: 1994–1997
Series 11: 1997 onwards

ENGINE:
Front longitudinal boxer four-cylinder – capacities ranging from 1351cc to 1969cc or four-cylinder in-line turbo diesel, 1929cc, mounted transversely *Power output:* from 90bhp to 150bhp (petrol); 90bhp (turbo diesel)

TRANSMISSION:
Five-speed gearbox

BODY STYLE:
Three-door hatchback

PERFORMANCE:
Top speed: from 111mph (178kph) to 135mph (216kph)

Alfa 164
1987–1998

ENGINE:
Front engine transversely mounted, four-cylinder in line or 60-degree V6 – capacities ranging from 1962cc to 2959cc or four-cylinder in line transversely mounted 2500cc turbo diesel. *Power output:* from 148bhp to 231bhp (petrol); 125bhp (turbo diesel)

TRANSMISSION:
Five or six-speed gearbox

BODY STYLE:
Four door saloon

PERFORMANCE:
Top speed: from 125mph (200kph) to 150mph (240kph)

The GTV6 at first retained the Alfetta GT's unusual instrument layout, albeit now with the rev-counter and speedometer having changed places; the gear lever now has a wooden knob to match the wood-rim steering wheel. (LAT)

staid-looking sedan, but in the coupé the relationship was dynamite. The engine had been transformed and the GTV6 met with rave reviews.' With a top speed of 127mph (205kph), this was an Alfa in the old tradition, even though it was clear that the gearchange was still giving trouble on some of the cars.

The character of the GTV6 is dominated by the V6 engine. Gorgeous-sounding, it has a howling, urgent soundtrack leagues apart from that of today's sanitised bread-and-butter V6s. Gutsy and chesty low down, the engine note edges towards a scream as revs build up: no wonder owners can be caught opening the

windows and flooring the throttle when passing through a tunnel or running alongside a tall wall. Flexible and with a flowing power delivery, it is an engine that you don't need to rev hard – other than for sheer aural pleasure. It's not hugely fast, but somehow that doesn't seem to matter.

The rest of the car can disappoint, suggesting that a 'four' may be a better bet if you can resist the allure of that sublime V6. There's a tendency to understeer, the ride is quite pitchy, and the steering – which tends to load up under cornering forces – is heavy enough to prompt thoughts of the desirability of power-assistance. High-speed cornering, as a consequence, demands a dose of muscle. And the gearchange? It's reasonable if the bushing is in good order and the linkage properly adjusted, but there's no great feel of precision, and the shift always has a certain sponginess about its action.

The Alfa 6 was discontinued in 1984, to be replaced by a V6 version of a new model, the Alfa 90, which was introduced as a replacement for the Alfetta. The V6 now used fuel injection rather than carburettors, and the body was a rather subtle reworking by Bertone of the now all-too-familiar Alfetta style, but with more luxurious fittings and fixtures.

Alfa admitted that the 90 was aimed at winning the company a larger share of the Mercedes market, so perhaps the model name hinted at its would-be target, the German company's new compact model, the 190. Certainly the top-of-the-range version had power steering, central locking, electric windows and seat

adjustment, and air-conditioning, with a top speed of 121mph (196kph), which was good for a heavy 27.4cwt (1390kg) saloon, even one fitted with a 2.5-litre V6.

In general the new engine, with its fuel injection, proved as successful and as popular as it had in the GTV6, but the familiar story of difficult gearshifts once more marred the picture, in spite of revised 'Isostatic' linkages intended to make the system easier to use. It was also true that reliability and simple build quality still had a long way to go to rival German standards, in a market sector where Alfa's name and image counted for much less. Within a year of its launch the 90 was joined by a re-jigged Giulietta, but soon afterwards Alfa took the decision, faced by the 90's lack of success, to terminate production of the car and concentrate on the new 75 model.

The Alfa 75, named in honour of the company's 75th anniversary under its original 'A.L.F.A.' designation, was

The Alfa 90 was a short-lived modernisation of the Alfetta. (LAT)

The Alfa Romeo 75 was a rejigged Giulietta launched to mark the company's 75th anniversary. (Alfa Romeo archives)

137mph (220kph). Finally, the 2-litre 'four' was made available in twin-spark form, as an alternative way of providing faster and more efficient combustion for greater economy and lower emissions. Alfa claimed that this version delivered more torque and used less fuel than the single-spark version, and it became an option on an increasing number of models.

By then, however, the old company, which had survived so many threats and challenges in its long history, had ceased to exist as an independent, albeit government-backed, organisation. The lack of development capital had now become almost terminal. Fiat and Ford moved in to squabble over the spoils in the mid-1980s, but negotiations ended in November 1986 with Fiat taking over

With the help of other Fiat models both Alfa plants were now working flat out

somewhat akin to an enlarged 33 in its appearance, but beneath the skin it was pure Alfetta/Giulietta. It was fitted with either the 1.8-litre version of the classic twin-cam 'four', or the 2.5-litre V6. The former had twin double-choke carburettors and a top speed of 116mph (187kph), while with the extra power available with the fuel-injected V6 the driver could persuade the car to change from understeer to oversteer on demand.

During the car's production run, a three-speed V6 automatic appeared, still good for a top speed of 130mph (209kph). This was joined at the top of the range by a faster and more powerful 2959cc version of the V6, with power up from 156bhp to 188bhp. This raised the top speed to

the last remaining sector of the Italian car industry to remain outside its ownership. It cost the giant car producer some £1 billion, and suggestions were made that the 33 range would be dropped, Pomigliano d'Arco would be closed, and future Alfas would be made on Fiat chassis, with Fiat engines and transmissions. It was already certain that the Alfa 75 would be the last rear-drive Alfa, the last Alfa to have the Alfetta driveline set-up, and the last genuinely 'Alfa' Alfa. The future seemed bleak and uncertain, even if the company was at

RIGHT:
The new brutalism: Zagato's limited production SZ was based on the 75 floorpan; only 1000 or so were made, plus no more than 250 of the open RZ version. (LAT)

The Alfa 164, here a Twin Spark, differed from the other 'Type 4' cars in not using the 'co-op' doors found in identical form on the Saab, Fiat and Lancia. (Alfa Romeo archives)

last financially secure. Nor was Alfa alone in appearing to have lost its old touch. Zagato's new SZ, based on 75 mechanicals, was as far away from the company's inspired designs of the past, from the original 1750 to the Giulietta and Giulia and the Junior Z, as it was possible to go. For the first time it introduced a New Brutalism into an Alfa design that made it look massive, heavy and sluggish, none of them qualities associated with Zagato designs of the past.

The first car to appear after the Fiat take-over was Alfa's Type 4 project, part of a big international collaboration between Alfa Romeo, Lancia, Fiat and Saab to share the costs of producing a common front-wheel-drive, big-car chassis, which would then be fitted with each company's mechanical parts and badged and marketed as one of its own models. In the Saab catalogue it appeared as the 9000, in Fiat's as the Croma, in Lancia's as the Thema, and finally, after long delays, as the Alfa Romeo 164.

Most agreed it had been worth the wait. The Alfa version of the Type 4 project was styled by Pininfarina, and it looked very different from the others. Moreover, it had the undeniable benefits of Alfa engines and running gear, which included four different power unit options: the twin-spark 1962cc four-cylinder engine now delivering 148 bhp; the 3-litre V6; a new 24-valve version of the last-named delivering a resounding 220 bhp; and a 2.4-litre turbo-diesel.

The front suspension featured MacPherson struts and coil springs, with wide lower wishbones and an anti-roll bar. The lower ends of the struts were deliberately angled forward to enable them to be mounted level with the front axles rather than above them, to allow a lower bonnet line. At the rear the 164 had a genuinely independent suspension, using struts, transverse arms, reaction rods and an anti-roll bar. The net result was a soft and comfortable ride, with impeccable handling at the price of a modest return to the old Alfa characteristics of initial body-roll on corners.

Much to the company's relief, the car was a real success. *Autocar* summed up the feelings of many when it assessed the 164 as 'a German car with personality', and the overall consensus was much more in keeping with the kind of reaction the company used to enjoy when a new model was unveiled. Alongside the 164, as the company entered the 1990s, was an updated 33 range, now available with a 1721cc version of the flat-four engine that was also offered on the last Sprint model before its demise. This larger power unit came in a standard 110bhp version, and as a 137bhp 16-valve. In this form the three versions – 33 saloon, Sportwagon estate and 4x4 – boasted top speeds in the 126–129mph (203–208kph) range.

At last the future seemed brighter. With the help of other Fiat Group models, both Alfa plants were at last working at full capacity, and in 1990

the company produced a profit, before the Italian market plunged into recession. Through a succession of difficult years it was clear that the Fiat take-over had come none too soon, but concerns were expressed as to whether or not new Alfas would have the vital qualities of their forebears, or be merely Fiats with different badges on the front.

In the end, perhaps the truth is something of a compromise. The Alfa Romeo 155 was the first entirely new design to emerge since the take-over, and was based on the chassis and running gear of the Fiat Tipo. The engines ranged from the old twin-cam 'four' in 1779cc form, but now with twin-spark ignition and developing 129bhp, through a Fiat-developed 1995cc twin-cam unit fitted with an Alfa-designed head and producing 143bhp, to the 2.5-litre Alfa V6 delivering 166bhp.

It seemed that the enduring Alfa characteristic body roll was back, as was engine noise in the smallest and

Alfa's interesting four-wheel-drive estate car based on the 33, the Sportwagon. (LAT)

The Alfa Romeo 145 started life with the ex-Sud flat-four as one of the engine systems, but this was soon dropped. (Alfa Romeo UK)

hardest-working version. Handling was good, and the finish of the car was better. Although there was still room for improvement, there were grounds for enthusiasts to hope that the combination of the best of Alfa Romeo with the best of the parent company's resources might yet prove to be a winning formula for the future. Unfortunately, despite the improvement in the company's finances, most customers were not convinced. The 155 looked promising on paper, but the reactions of those who tried early models were scathing. Later chassis revisions helped, to the point where in 1992 *What Car?* said that 'enthusiasts feared that the 155 would betray its Fiat Tipo underpinnings, but they needn't worry. It's sporty, good to drive, but lacks the elegance of the bigger 164.'

Since then a whole series of Fiat Alfas has emerged on to the market, with progressively more appeal and

progressively more commercial success. These began with the 145 and 146 sporting hatchbacks and the new and sharply styled Spider and GTV, all of them – like the 155 – based on the Tipo floorpan. Each of these new designs won increasingly popular acclaim, but the car that began the real renaissance of Alfa's commercial appeal was the highly successful 156, which won the company its first Car of the Year award in 1998.

Both the 145 and 146 were offered with a choice of 1.8-litre and 2.0-litre 16-valve Twin Spark engines. Although these were both twin overhead-cam four-cylinder designs according to the traditional Alfa configuration, they actually shared none of their principal dimensions with the company's earlier engines. Their complex and sophisticated design seemed a world away from the ingenious and high-quality but firmly traditional craftsmanship of the old days; but one measure of their increased efficiency was an appreciably higher power output from 1747cc than was delivered by the 1962cc engine fitted to the 2000 models two decades earlier. The larger engine also had a twin balancer-shaft system intended to damp out the characteristic vibrations of a four-cylinder unit.

Performance of these models was undeniably well up to Alfa standards, with the 145 reaching 129mph (206kph) in 1.8-litre form, and 136mph (210kph) in 2-litre form. For the 146, maximum speeds were slightly higher at 130mph (208kph) and 136mph (214kph) respectively. Perhaps more remarkably, this level of performance came at around 60–70

per cent of the fuel consumption of their illustrious predecessors.

As a result of changes like these, discerning a historical lineage became much more difficult, and separating the Alfa bloodline from that of Fiat all but impossible. On the other hand, the whole range was able to provide as varied a choice as before, with many of the new engines shared between different models, just as was done in the past. For example, the award-winning 156 shared the 1.8-litre and 2.0-litre Twin Spark engines with its smaller stablemates and inherited its Tipo-derived chassis from the 155. Only one glorious, unrepentant exception to this corporate break with the past remained: one of the engine options for the 156 was the 2.5-litre V6, which

The Alfa Romeo 156. (Alfa Romeo UK)

provided a direct link with the Alfetta GTV6 and the Alfa 90.

Even here, though, there was change in plenty. Instead of the single overhead camshaft per cylinder bank of the previous V6, using horizontal pushrods and rockers to actuate the exhaust valves, the engine reverted to the older Alfa configuration of double overhead camshafts for each cylinder bank, making four in all. This time there were 24 valves for improved breathing, and the combustion chambers were flattened to increase the area of the valve openings, while the electronic 'drive-by-wire' throttle was adapted from those used in Formula 1. The six-speed manual

gearbox harked back to those fitted to the original Alfa Romeo 33 sports racing prototypes of 1967.

Largest engine in the range was a 3-litre version of the V6, delivering 220bhp at 6,300rpm and a massive 199lb ft of torque at 5,000rpm. This provided an extra performance option, alongside the 2.0-litre Twin Spark, for the rakish new Spider and GTV coupé.

In other respects, the Fiat take-over has been more marked, with chassis, floorpan and running gear inherited from the company's other models. In a sense this is merely an extension of the process that Alfa Romeo had

The Alfa Romeo GTV 3.0-litre 24-valve V6. (Alfa Romeo UK)

The 166 is the latest Fiat-era Alfa. (Alfa Romeo UK)

already initiated when it became, along with Saab, one of the two non-Fiat companies to sign up to the Type 4 project.

The next car in the Alfa Romeo line-up, the flagship 166, took the theme a stage further. The design used an adaptation of the front suspension wishbone from the 156, in conjunction with a new multi-link independent rear suspension. The car was offered with three engine options: the 2-litre Twin Spark four-cylinder unit, and 2.5-litre and 3-litre V6s. Both the smaller engines followed Alfa tradition by having five-speed manual gearboxes, but the 3-litre unit was fitted with a six-speed transmission. By any standards the 166 was an impressive and sophisticated design with a whole raft of unusual features, including an automatic transmission option for the

V6 versions which could adapt itself both to the driver's style of handling the car at any time and to the road conditions encountered on a particular journey, with the option of reverting to manual control when this mode was selected.

Were cars like these still Alfas in character? While road tests and design analysis features could provide facts and figures and opinions in plenty, the answer to such a subjective question was bound to depend in the end on personal preferences and first-hand experience. Certainly today's buyers, whatever their feelings on the pedigree of the cars, are offered all kinds of inducements which earlier generations of Alfa owners would have given a great deal to enjoy. These have included improved anti-theft security, factory-guaranteed

The rear view of the sophisticated 166 – but does the prominent Alfa badge on the bootlid reflect the car's true character?

used Alfas, and – with a special irony – enhanced standards of quality and corrosion protection. The idea of a three-year, 60,000-mile warranty, and a corrosion protection warranty valid for eight years, would have made Alfisti from the 60s and 70s feel they had died and passed on to automotive heaven.

Now these benefits were being offered with technical sophistications like cruise and traction control, satellite navigation, and clever adaptive transmissions. Was this what the buyers wanted, and did the policy work in commercial terms? During the late 1990s it appeared that the answer was 'yes', with the company claiming huge improvements in sales over the figures immediately preceding the Fiat take-over.

Yet some changes have been more significant than others. As far as the 166 was concerned, only the engines were being made at the old Alfa plant at Arese near Milan; the cars themselves were assembled at a different factory, near Fiat's headquarters at Turin. Immediately this posed the question as to whether these latest creations, still proudly bearing the Alfa badge, were genuine modern equivalents. Perhaps the best answer lies in the succession of models produced at the start of the 21st century, in the years leading up to the 100th anniversary of the company's founding. At worst these could be said to be Fiats with a more sporting character, at best Alfas for a new age, designed, engineered, and produced with a new acceptance of commercial realities.

Alfas
for a new century

Perhaps the first model to show this combination of up-to-date design which owed little to the past, with close links to the character and philosophy of previous Alfas, was the 147. This was a logical extension of the smaller Alfa theme established by its 145 and 146 predecessors, and made its appearance precisely on cue at the turn of the new century. Its lines were sporty and exciting where the 145 and 146 were utilitarian and inoffensive. Its sleek and compact

three-door body was given a highly symbolic restyling of the characteristic Alfa front end. Instead of the triangular shield used on the current range at the time, this reverted to what was called the 'Villa d'Este' grille. What was meant by this was the tall and narrow grille opening found on early post-war Alfas, in particular in the opulent six-cylinder 2500 Super Sport coupé bodied by Carrozzeria Touring in 1952, which symbolised the company's recovery from wartime ruin.

The neat and compact Alfa 147 – seen here in three door form with the prominent 'Villa d'Este' grille – proved to be a highly desirable package with a great deal of driver appeal and a good basis for sporting variations.

Alfa Spider and GTV
Current

ENGINE:
Front longitudinal four–cylinder in–line engine – capacity 1970cc JTS (Jet Thrust Stochiometric OR 3179cc V6 petrol engine. *Power output:* 121bhp (Four-cylinder JTS Lusso); 165bhp (V6 petrol engine)

TRANSMISSION:
Five speed gearbox (1970cc engine) or six-speed gearbox (V6)

BODY STYLE:
Two–door sports car or GT coupé

PERFORMANCE:
Top speed: GTV: 137mph (219kph) – two-litre JTS; 155mph (248kph) – three-litre V6; Spider: 134mph (214kph) – two-litre; JTS: 150mph (240kph) – three–litre V6

Alfa 147
Current

ENGINE:
Front mounted four–cylinder in–line engine – capacity 1598cc or 1970cc petrol or 1910cc four–cylinder 16V turbo diesel. *Power output:* ranging from 77bhp (1.6 petrol engine) to 113bhp (2.0 litre petrol engine)

TRANSMISSION:
Five–speed manual gearbox or five–speed semi–automatic Selespeed sequential transmission

BODY STYLE:
Three– or five–door hatchback

PERFORMANCE:
Top speed: ranges from 115mph (184kph) (1.6-litre Twin Spark 16V) to 129mph (206kph) (2.0-litre Twin Spark 16V)

Once again, thanks to front-wheel drive and all-round independent suspension, carefully engineered to provide top-quality handling and with a standard of build quality sadly missing from all too many post-war Alfas, the 147 was a design which made enthusiasts sit up and take notice. As with its 156 predecessor three years before, it won the Car of the Year award for 2001, when five-door versions were added to the range, and as sales increased more and more engine options were offered to provide performance in plenty. From the viewpoint of Alfa's own traditions, though, the most remarkable had to be the diesel option. Diesel Alfas in the old days had been something of an afterthought – the combination of high fuel economy and indifferent performance was not something generally associated with the company name, and sales had been less than spectacular.

The start of the new millennium had seen big changes in the market for diesel cars, however. Thanks to new technology which had tamed the knock and vibration for which diesels were notorious, allied to turbo-charging and improved injection systems to transform their performance, the popularity of diesel cars had soared. In Europe as a whole, diesel cars were expected to outsell petrol-engined versions by 2007; and even in the UK, where diesel fuel was actually more expensive than unleaded petrol, gains in the market share of diesel cars have been spectacular. This was the sector at which Alfa was aiming when it equipped the 147 and 156 with its JTD high-pressure Unijet 1.9-litre diesel engines featuring common rail all-electronic direct injection, a technology pioneered by Fiat in the late 1980s.

In its original form the 1.9-litre diesel developed 115bhp, enough to give the 147 a top speed of 115mph (185kph) and the power to reach 62mph (100kph) from a standing start in 9.9 seconds. Fitted in the 156, it delivered the same top speed, but, as befitted a larger and heavier body, an acceleration time to 62mph just 0.4 seconds slower. This was encouraging

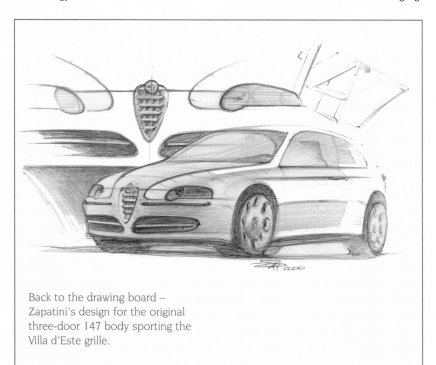

Back to the drawing board – Zapatini's design for the original three-door 147 body sporting the Villa d'Este grille.

enough, but better news for Alfa fans came with the announcement of a more powerful Multijet version of the engine featuring twin overhead cams and four valves per cylinder, boosting output to 140bhp at 4,000rpm and torque of 224lb ft at half this speed. Performance of the 147 JTD was increased to a top speed of 129mph (208kph) and the 0–62mph time fell to 9.1 seconds.

Still very much current, these power units feature sophisticated technology that is the direct equivalent of the ground-breaking twin-cam hemispherical combustion chamber Alfa engines of the distant past. The Unijet unit's high-pressure injection system uses a pilot injection to raise temperature and pressure inside the cylinder, to improve combustion efficiency when the main fuel charge is injected later in the induction stroke. The Multijet design extends this principle to a series of smaller injections, with the aim of ensuring a more gradual and more complete combustion process, to give better performance with reduced noise, vibration, and emissions.

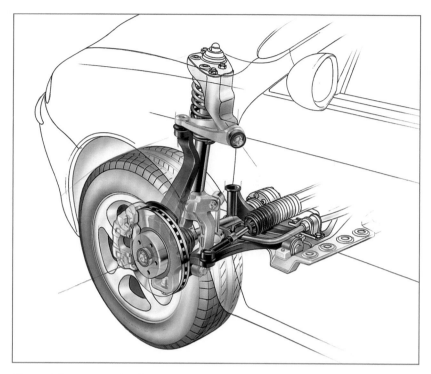

The Multijet engine also features details such as new inlet and exhaust manifolds, steel connecting rods and crankshaft, and modified pistons with an internal channel to carry oil to the little-end bearings. The new injectors

Double wishbone front suspension for the Alfa 147 – the car's impressive list of handling improvement features includes braking system distribution control to apportion effort between front and rear, and anti-slip regulation to maintain optimum grip under acceleration.

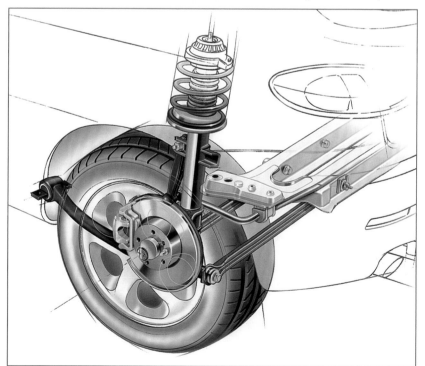

Independent 147 rear suspension uses McPherson strut configuration – additional handling improvement features include a torque regulation system when moving down through the gears and an optional dynamic stability control system to compensate for understeering or oversteering tendencies.

Alfa radiator grilles

One of the features of the current range of Alfa Romeo models is the switch to the 'Villa d'Este' shape of radiator grille, billed as a link with the company's glorious past. Even though the link does genuinely exist, it actually has much less to do with the classic Alfas of pre-war days like the immortal 1750s or the straight-eight 2300s, the Monzas or the P3s or any of the other models which won the company its splendid reputation. What the shape *does* hark back to is the much greyer and grimmer conditions of the early post-war years, when Alfa Romeo was struggling to survive the effects of wartime bombing and the partial disappearance of its traditional customers in favour of higher-volume production and an altogether more price-conscious market.

Unlike companies such as Rolls-Royce, where a real attempt was made to develop a style which could be applied to all the company's models from the very earliest days, the Alfas of the 1920s and 1930s avoided a rigid corporate style altogether. In any case, the common practice of building a bare chassis on which the company or the customer would commission a specialist coachbuilder to fit the actual bodywork, meant that the only part of a car which could be designed to a particular shape tended to be the front end. Hence the Rolls-Royce radiator which spanned the decades from the Silver Ghosts of Edwardian days to their current successors.

Alfa's approach was much more utilitarian. In the early days, the radiator shape merely reflected the cross-section of the shape enclosed by the bonnet, which was itself governed by the dimensions of the engine. Where a continuing style did emerge, from the six-cylinder 1500

and 1750 Sports, Super Sports and Gran Sports onwards, the radiator shape was very slightly reminiscent of the Georgian-portico shape of the Rolls radiator – broadly speaking a rectangle topped by a shallow triangle. This was the configuration for the sports cars and the eight cylinder models which succeeded them, the racing P3s and the hybrid Monzas, all of which began to establish a clear visual identity for successive Alfa Romeo models. However, the style failed to endure. The later production car designs of the 1930s were given a new style, with a rectangular radiator with rounded corners, a style which lasted to the early post-war cars.

Only with the first of the newly styled post-war Alfas, the 6C 2500 'Freccia d'Oro' or 'Golden Arrow' of 1947, closely based mechanically on its pre-war stable-mates, did the shape of the radiator change. Gone was the semi-rectangular grille which had served on a series of different models for an entire decade – instead, the car sported a radiator shaped in outline like the Norman shields on the Bayeux tapestry. A long narrow triangle, sweeping down from a narrow top with rounded corners to a point at the bottom held within it a series of crossbars protecting the radiator proper.

This was the first appearance of the shape which was now renamed after the 'Villa d'Este'. Apart from choosing a rarer variant rather than the original – 'Villa d'Este' was first applied in the automotive sense to a Touring bodied variation on the Super Sport theme which first appeared in 1949 (according to Alfa's website) on in 1952 (according to the company's official history) – the shape was perpetuated on the unitary-construction 1900 range whereby the company dipped a corporate toe into

the chilly waters of the mass market for the first time, and which first appeared in much greater numbers from 1950.

It was also seen on the original Giulietta design of the mid-1950s, and the Giulia range which succeeded it. Only through the later decades did it put on weight and progressively fatten and flatten into the more conventional shield shape – effectively a new style altogether. In finally reverting to the earlier design, Alfa was simply following a motor industry trend of a different kind – but why the 'Villa d'Este' and not the 'Freccia d'Oro'? At least the 'Golden Arrow' name symbolises speed and luxury – not for nothing was it carried by the London to Paris Pullman train of the old Southern Railway. The Villa d'Este title symbolises a mixture of luxury and licence, imprisonment and debauchery, vaulting ambition and the punishment of fate, a far less appealing prescription for those who look for the original derivation of the title (see page 165).

work to smaller time limits, with 150 microseconds between successive injections and a complex and responsive control system to cope with different combinations of engine torque, speed, and temperature. At low temperatures and torque requirements the injection system delivers three charges of fuel into each cylinder: two small pulses and one larger pulse. As the torque requirement increases, injections are limited to one small pulse and one large one. At high speeds and torque requirements a single charge suffices, while at higher temperatures the system can deliver one small injection followed by a large one and then another small charge in a single timed sequence.

For Alfa fans, such as the editorial team of *Auto Italia*, these highly sophisticated diesels are still – well – diesels, and for the time being the jury is still very much out. As one of their writers explained: 'Anyone with an ounce of style is a fan of the Alfa 147; it is without doubt one of the most fabulously desirable family cars of the century, never mind the decade. It does have its faults – the ride is imperfect and the entry-level performance figures unremarkable – but the superlative styling and sensuous interior are way ahead of other cars in its class. I yearn to own one. Yet I was wary of trying the 1.9 16v M-Jet. Sure, the 140bhp Multijet is a big improvement on the agricultural 8v 1.9JTD – quieter, smoother, stronger and less suited to ploughing fields – but it's still very much a diesel. Alfa might be leading the diesel revolution, first with its common rail engines and then its ground-breaking Multijet technology, but some manufacturers are now building diesels which are hard to distinguish from petrol models. And Alfa isn't yet one of them'.

The other major change of the early 2000s for both the 156 and 147 was another blast from the past: the introduction of a lighter and

substantially more powerful version called the GTA, harking right back to the *Gran Turismo Alleggerita* Giulias and Giuliettas of the late 1960s onwards. First to appear, in 2000, was the 156 GTA, powered by a 3.2-litre, four-camshaft, 24-valve, all-aluminium version of Alfa's V6. The 147 GTA, using the same engine, made its debut in the spring of 2003. With a peak power output of 250bhp and 213lb ft of torque, this was a new variation on an old Alfa formula, providing a top speed in the 156, in sixth gear, of 155mph (250kph), and a 0–62mph time of just 6.3 seconds. As with the old GTAs, this was a way of combining a potent and attractive road car with a viable basis for a competition machine. Alfa won the 2002 European Touring Car Challenge with the 156 GTA, which also gave Fabrizio Giovanardi the drivers' title.

On the road, *Auto Italia* gave the car high praise: 'The first thing you notice is that this front-wheel drive saloon does not understeer. On a racetrack it may be different but I simply could not unsettle the GTA on the road. Think about it, front-wheel drive and 250bhp – you should not be able to give full bore exiting a roundabout

Alfa 156
Current

ENGINE:
Front longitudinal four-cylinder in-line engine – capacity from 1598cc TS (Twin Spark) to 1970cc JTS (Jet Thrust Stochiometric) or 2387cc five-cylinder in-line JTD diesel. *Power output:* 88bhp (Four-cylinder Twin Spark petrol engine); 129bhp (Five-cylinder JTD diesel); 121bhp (Four-cylinder 1970cc JTS Selespeed)

TRANSMISSION:
Five or six-speed gearbox or five-speed semi-automatic Selespeed sequential transmission

BODY STYLE:
Four-door saloon or five-door Sportwagon estate

PERFORMANCE:
Top speed: 124mph (199kph) (Twin Spark); 137mph (219kph) – JTS Selespeed; 140mph (224kph) – JTD diesel

Six cylinders, four overhead camshafts, 24 valves – the traditional Alfa prescription as applied to the 3.2-litre V6 power units of the GTA versions of the 147 and 156.

Seen in the current version of the 156 front end (top and middle), the new 'Villa d'Este grille' seems a much less radical change than the version used on the 147. Compared with the original 156 grille shape, as retained for the time being on the 156GTA (bottom), the shape is only slightly narrower, with a thinner surround and prominent horizontal bars, and a long way from the original of more than 50 years ago.

on a wet road without dire consequences. Ah, you say, it's the electronics, and indeed the GTA is fitted with ASR (anti-slip regulation). Traction control systems on poorly designed cars are horrible, often giving unwanted intervention in throttle control and as a result grip loss. This GTA is one of the few cars where you don't feel compelled to switch off the ASR. As a direct result of racing and winning in the European Touring Car Championships the many suspension enhancements made to the GTA mean grip levels are very high and wet weather ability is superlative; the ASR warning lamp glows softly, killing instability due to aquaplaning, but otherwise remains mostly inactive. Indeed, grip is so massive that even under emergency braking you are hard pressed to provoke the ABS to engage.

'As a result of such grip, handling on real roads is superb; whereas a car like the Fiat Coupé Turbo feels on the ragged edge if you exploit its 220bhp, the GTA goes where you want, when you want. At 1.75 turns lock to lock, steering is racing sharp, and the car is always on the move. It feels as if it has built-in instability like a Eurofighter, which needs to be tamed by electronics, but the result is extraordinary agility. Ride is inevitably somewhat harsh but this is a performance orientated car, a fact reinforced by an aggressive stance which is 20mm lower than lesser 156s, combined with an integral front splitter and flared wheel arches which extend to body-coloured side skirts.'

By 2003 the 156 was in for still more change. Apart from an ambitious Giugiaro restyling exercise which began by revamping the front end to a more aggressive shape, including the Villa d'Este radiator grille, and a profile which swept back to a neater rear end with flush bumpers, the 156 was also given an entirely new top-range power unit to replace the old 2.5-litre petrol V6. In common with the spirit of the times, this was yet

What's in a name?

To confuse matters still further over the derivation of the new design feature on the latest generation of Alfas (see page 162) the name of Villa d'Este was given to two great houses, not one. The first was a residence built in the village of Tivoli, some 20 miles to the east of Rome during the mid-15th century for Cardinal Ippolito d'Este, after whom it was named. Apart from being a prince of the Church – he had been appointed a bishop at the age of 2, an archbishop at 10 and a cardinal at 30 – he was the son of the notorious Lucrezia Borgia, daughter of Pope Alexander VI and wife to Alfonso I, Duke of Ferrara, and his parentage made him a prime candidate to succeed his grandfather on the papal throne. His ambitions were dashed by the appointment of Julius III as the new pontiff, and Julius was careful to prevent his rival from ever presenting a serious challenge to his position.

He appointed d'Este to be Governor of Tivoli in 1550. Since Governors could not leave the provinces they governed without permission, this effectively made him a prisoner on his own magnificent estate, and he spent the remaining 22 years of his life constructing the most splendid gardens with complex systems of fountains designed and constructed by specialist engineers. Later these fell into disuse but during the last 20 years a determined restoration programme has begun the mammoth task of restoring the Villa d'Este to its former glory.

The second house to carry the name was built only two decades later on the western shore of Lake Como in the north of Italy. Originally named the Villa del Garrovo after a stream which flowed into the lake close to the house, it was eventually sold in 1815 to Caroline of Brunswick, the estranged wife of Britain's Prince Regent, the future King George IV. One of her distant ancestors had been a Guelfo d'Este, and she renamed the house the 'New Villa d'Este' in his honour, and added a library and a theatre to the house. Her scandalous conduct attracted the attentions of the Prince's agents who were assembling evidence for the forthcoming Royal divorce, and in 1821 she was tried unsuccessfully for adultery on her return to London.

She was excluded from her husband's coronation and died less than three weeks later amid rumours of a hereditary illness, a brain tumour or deliberate poisoning. The house was sold and passed through a series of different owners until it was opened as the luxurious Hotel Villa d'Este in 1873 after expensive and extensive renovations. It remains a hotel to this day, with its own collection of priceless sixteenth century paintings and sculptures, surrounded by a large park with caves, grottoes and fountains.

another diesel, this time the 2.4-litre, five-cylinder, turbocharged, 20-valve Multijet unit, pushing out 175bhp at 4,000rpm and having peak torque of 284lb ft at 2,000rpm – enough, according to the company, to push the car to 62mph (100kph) from a

Alfas back where they belong: Tarquini's works 156GTA leading a trio of arch-rival BMWs in the 2003 Touring Car Championship, which Alfa won in a nail-biting finish to the season.

standing start in 8.3 seconds, and endow it with a top speed of 140mph (225kph). Slightly less happy, according to some enthusiasts, were revisions to the suspension settings, with lower friction and softer damper settings to improve ride comfort.

Much of the visuals owed their inspiration to the Alfa Brera concept car from the shows of the previous year, with comprehensive reworking by Georgetto Giugiaro and his Ital Design studio. The tidying-up around the tail-lamp enclosures was rather more subtle, but the overall impression was of a leaner, more elegant and aerodynamic shape, though with a strong resemblance to the earlier version.

All these exciting changes were by now leaving the top of the range 166 increasingly isolated. In the opinion of many Alfa fans its styling in particular was due for a facelift to bring it into a closer relationship with the rest of the

family, and late in 2003 it was given the full treatment, with the by now mandatory Villa d'Este grille and larger headlamps but the rest of the bodywork mostly left alone. The result was a car still recognisable as a 166, but a 166 now much more in harmony with the current range of Alfas. Other changes were limited principally to revised suspension settings to reduce diving under braking and body roll in corners – two enduring behavioural links with illustrious Alfas of the past, but less appropriate in today's much more demanding performance car market.

It was also given a new engine line-up, with a choice of four power units. These included, at the upper end, both the 3.2-litre version of the V6 and a still powerful and responsive 3.0-litre 24-valve version, harnessed to the Sportronic automatic transmission. For *Auto Express* both were undeniably attractive. In their view 'Alfas are bought for their

engines, and this 3.0-litre proves why. As well as being powerful and sounding great, it works perfectly with the four-speed auto box to make overtaking effortless. For swifter progress, you can select sports mode or change manually using the console-mounted gearlever. With 220bhp on tap and a healthy 265Nm of torque, the 166 sprints from 0–62mph in 8.6 seconds. But for breathtaking performance, you'll want the all-new 3.2-litre flagship. Taking its tuneful 240bhp engine from the scorching 156 GTA and fitted with a six-speed manual gearbox, it covers the 0–62mph dash in only 7.4 seconds, and pulls eagerly throughout the rev range.'

Other styling changes to update the appeal of the car included new headlamp clusters located on either side of the ventilation grilles, and fog lights built into the chin spoiler. Rear-end revisions were carried out to improve aerodynamics and reduce

drag. Backing up the two 3-litre engines was the direct injection 150bhp 2-litre Twin Spark with a 16-valve head, and a 220bhp 2.5-litre version of the V6. Does the new prescription work? When the press came to grips with the revamped model, it earned mixed reviews. *Car* praised the new 3.2 V6 as 'torquey, smooth, sounds great' – almost an ideal description of the old, traditional Alfas – and hailed the revised and stiffer rear suspension for its role in 'reducing the untoward body movement that has until now limited the cornering pleasure, and [doing so] without messing up the ride'.

The problem, in their correspondent's view, was not in the handling itself, but in the responses when the driver tried to use the power of the engine to accelerate in anything other than a straight line. 'The 3.2 pulls strongly from 2,000rpm and really gets going at 4,000, at which point torque steer makes an appearance, even with the

Alfa's racing team and fans celebrate winning the 2003 Touring Car Championship by a single point from their closest competitors – the BMW team – at the end of the final event of the series.

Alfa GT

Current

ENGINE:
Front longitudinal four-cylinder in-line engine – capacity 1970cc JTS (Jet Thrust Stochiometric or 1910cc four-cylinder in-line turbo diesel or 3179cc V6 petrol engine. *Power output:* 122bhp (Four-cylinder JTS petrol engine); 110bhp (turbo diesel); 176bhp (V6 petrol engine)

TRANSMISSION:
Five- or six-speed gearbox or five-speed semi-automatic Selespeed sequential transmission

BODY STYLE:
Two-door GT coupé

PERFORMANCE:
Top speed: 134mph (214kph) – four-cylinder petrol engines; 130mph (207kph) – turbo diesel; 151mph (242kph) – V6 petrol

ASR system active. When you start to make use of this fine engine's ability, the limitations of front-wheel drive soon come to the fore as the tyres scrabble for grip. So Alfa's recently rediscovered enthusiasm for all things sporting doesn't fully manifest itself in the 166 3.2. That said, it's with the 3.2 engine that the 166 is at its best, rather than the 2.0-litre four or the 3.0-litre V6s. With the car's refinement now matched by elegant looks and hefty reserves of power and torque, backed up by manly brakes, a light and precise six-speed transmission, and generally good ride and handling, this is the executive saloon for the executive who wants to stand out.' Equally praised were the roomy interior and the cavernous boot, though the magazine complained of a certain lack of support in the front seats.

Altogether, the opening of the 21st century has proved to be an exciting time for Alfa enthusiasts. In spite of a progressive loosening of the

traditions of the past, the company has striven to cope with the demands of the future in a subtle combination of the Alfa philosophy along with, or sometimes in spite of, much more up-to-date engineering. There have been other, stronger, links with the past, though, such as the use of one successful design as the basis for a widening range of new models. In the 1960s it had been the Giulia. In the first decade of the new century the role of basis for the new range was to be played by the innovative and still successful 156.

In its own right, the design had proved a trump card in competition. As the end of the 2003 competition season approached with the onset of autumn, the works 156 GTAs had turned out to be so successful on the track that Alfa Romeo were in serious contention for the year's European Touring Car Drivers' Championship. However, this was no mere promenade in the park against unchallenging opposition. This had

proved to be a closely fought contest from the beginning, against the formidable BMWs. So tough was the contest that in spite of a string of six seasons in succession where the Italian cars had come home with a growing collection of silverware, as the teams assembled on their home turf of Monza for the final event in the series the smart money was edging towards a bet on the Munich cars taking the title this time round.

Alfa driver Gabriele Tarquini had reached the start of this closing race on precisely the same points as his BMW opposite number, Jörg Müller. The very slight edge apparently enjoyed by the German team was reflected in Müller having taken pole position after a less than inspiring performance by the Italians. For those praying for an Alfa victory, the run-up to the race could hardly have been worse. Much was expected from the

hiring of Grand Prix driver Giancarlo Fisichella to play a starring role in the team's fortunes, but he was to come unstuck in a big way during practice. His spectacular crash shattered his car beyond all hope of repair, and if that alone were not enough to dampen the hopes of Alfa fans, Tarquini and a third Alfa driver, Nicola Larini, managed to compound his bad luck by doing exactly the same, if rather less spectacularly. Between them, they had reduced the works entry from five cars to two. Only a heroic all-night repair job managed to put one of the wrecks back into fighting trim in time for the race, thereby raising the team strength to three. The best they could hope for was to be narrowly beaten rather than comprehensively thrashed.

In reality, the outcome was in some ways a re-run of the great Nuvolari win in the Alfa P3 against the might

Alfa's current versions of the GTV coupé (opposite) and Spider (above) share a much closer family resemblance than their predecessors dating back to the 1960s, thanks to a sharply wedge-shaped body embellished by a geological fault-line stretching back from the front headlamps to the rear deck.

Petrol – or diesel?

One of the clearest breaks with established Alfa tradition since the Fiat takeover has been the much greater prominence given to diesel variants throughout the model range. For a company where diesels had rarely figured in the line-up before, and had rarely qualified for more than a footnote in its history, this was a major policy shift and reflected the greater appeal of diesels with improved engine design, greater economy and improved environmental credentials which had become well established over the closing years of the 20th century.

The danger, as always for any maker specializing in cars for the enthusiast market, was that the new customers who might be successfully wooed by including diesel-powered versions in the choice presented to them, might be more than outweighed by the traditional buyers who might prefer to look elsewhere by what they might perceive as the company's failure to keep faith with its traditions. It remains a difficult balancing act for any car manufacturer to carry out successfully, especially in a market sector so dominated by engineering and sporting tradition. At a time when the embracing of compression ignition engines might be seized as an example of the Fiat ownership imposing its own ideas and priorities on the Alfa subsidiary, how successful has the company been?

Some drivers find a diesel version a welcome addition to the appeal of the latest Alfas. So far as the BBC's *Top Gear Buyer's Guide* was concerned, both the 1.9 litre and 2.4 litre versions of the diesels were 'both well up to class standards for power and economy'. On the other hand, *Top Gear* presenter James May was less convinced, at least in the case of the diesel versions of the GT

coupe. He admitted the diesels sounded 'quite nice' and even called them 'remarkably good', and praised them as 'gutsy and economical' but went on to criticize them as more suitable for a Ford Mondeo and complained about their abundance of torque as being inappropriate for a performance car.

Others were more responsive to the newer designs of diesels and their genuine advantages over the previous generation. The *Daily Telegraph* reviewed the first of the later Common Rail diesel engines, the 'in-line four-cylinder unit in which the M-JET system is combined with a new control system that increases the number of injections in the cylinder, assuring more gradual combustion, with surprising results: extraordinary power and torque, reduced emissions, improved fuel economy, all combined with remarkable refinement both in terms of noise and vibration. The M-JET system (that) permits multiple injections for increased fuel economy and even more brilliant performance'.

Even *Top Gear* had a good word to say about the optional new five-cylinder diesel available on the 156. 'There's a new engine in the range too. It has five cylinders, 20 valves, a displacement of 2.4 litres, 175bhp and a huge 284lb ft of torque. Yes, it's a diesel. One of the new generation of multi-jet JTD engines that will appear in other Fiat Group cars in the near future. And it's a beaut. Power delivery is smooth and muscular. Refinement is high, while noise levels are low'. Ironically, these were originally Fiat engines, later developed with General Motors for joint use. And the idea that Alfas may soon share engines with the likes of Astras and Vectras will hardly please loyal fans.

of the German Mercedes and Auto Union teams in the 1935 German GP. Against all the odds, the 156 GTAs delivered the goods by a narrow but definite margin. In spite of a huge first lap pile-up that took out eight of the entrants, the Alfa team survived. Roberto Colciago's GTA crossed the line in the lead, but was disqualified for having collided with Dirk Müller earlier in the event. Fortunately James Thompson, another of the team drivers, was in second place to take over the winner's position on the rostrum, followed by a mixture of works and privateer GTAs in the next three places. Jörg Müller had been heading for a convincing third place, but, in another echo of Nuvolari's victory, had been forced to retire on the penultimate lap with a puncture. After this excitement, the second race was more of a procession. This time Müller finished in first place, followed by Coronel and Tarquini in GTAs, a result which saw Alfa Romeo and Tarquini taking the seventh successive title by just a single point.

In addition to mid-life updates of the still appealing Spider and GTV, the other big news for Alfa fans during 2004 has been another string to the Alfa bow, once again based on the 156. This is the Alfa Romeo GT, which made its first appearance at the Frankfurt Show in the autumn of 2003. Unlike the parent saloon, this sleek two-door coupé was styled by Bertone in a way which – perhaps to reassure those most likely to buy it – re-emphasised the traditional Alfa personality rather more emphatically than usual. From the chrome grille, the body curves sweep back over a carefully shaped bonnet to close coupled bodywork and a subtly shaped tail-end treatment.

In terms of interior styling, though, the GT takes another step away from the spartan interiors of the Alfas of old. Recent models have been providing more and more comfort and appeal in terms of the Italian flair for design, and the GT provides deeply shrouded instruments, solid fittings, and the option of soft and fragrant leather upholstery in upmarket versions. The fat-rimmed three-spoke steering wheel is another link with the golden past, and the specification includes xenon headlamps, traction control, and anti-lock brakes.

Most who have tried the GT have praised its handling and responses as being very much those of a traditional Italian sports machine, improved by the clearest evidence of modern engineering and clever design. Where suspicions intrude, these mainly concern the company's claim that within the exterior of a smart two-door coupé, a full size five-seat saloon with a capacious load space to match is hiding as a pleasant surprise for customers once the ink on the cheque is dry. Rear seats prove barely adequate for two, in fact, and folding the seats forward to provide the claimed load space means it is possible to have luggage space or extra passengers, but not at the same time.

That said, the car has won praise all round for its driving qualities. As originally introduced, it was offered with the 2-litre JTS petrol unit and the 1.9-litre Multijet diesel as engine options. James May of *Top Gear* magazine was in no doubt which choice he preferred: 'The diesel is remarkably good and even sounds quite nice. It's also very gutsy and economical. And I still hate it. It would be great in a Mondeo, and I know Alfa diesels have been common for years in their homeland, but to me it's just not quite right. At the risk of sounding bloody minded, it produces too much torque for a car whose neck you expect (and want) to have to wring. So best wait for the Autumn and the 3.2-litre 24v V6 as found in the 156 GTA (though slightly retuned and with 240bhp). This, too, essentially produces too much torque, and a brutally driven 3.2 GT will scrabble around alarmingly under power. Drive around this problem, however, and you arrive at the most sonorous of any engine's upper reaches. This V6 is still one of the most charismatic bits of machinery in production.' Along with the V6, the

Alfa 166
Current

ENGINE:
Front longitudinal four-cylinder in-line engine – capacity 1970cc JTS (Jet Thrust Stochiometric or 2387cc five-cylinder in-line turbo diesel or V6 petrol engines from 1996cc to 2959cc. *Power output:* 155bhp (Four-cylinder JTS petrol engine); 136bhp (turbo diesel); 205bhp (1996cc V6 petrol engine); 226bhp (2959cc V6 petrol engine)

TRANSMISSION:
Six-speed gearbox or Sportronic automatic transmission with sequential control

BODY STYLE:
Four-door saloon

PERFORMANCE:
Top speed: 125mph (202kph) – 1970cc JTS petrol engines; 151mph (243kph) – 2959cc V6

A new shape for the future? Side view of Alfa's new GT coupé shows lines which would not be entirely out of place on an Audi or BMW design.

1.8-litre Twin Spark engine will appear at the bottom of the engine options list from the autumn of 2004, though most enthusiasts are likely to go for one of the more powerful units.

Meanwhile, some Alfa enthusiasts have criticised the GT design for relying too heavily on the heritage card to trump the opposition's hands in today's tough marketing conditions. The throwback grille design has been panned for being too large and unsubtle to suit the rest of the design, and the much vaunted reshaping of the 156 is seen by many as little more than a two-door cosmetic reskinning job. For those who remain unconvinced by the new GT, the ideal shape of things to come is better epitomised by a more traditional Alfa model in its latest incarnation – the two-door coupé GTV as revamped in mid-2003.

Seen from above, the GT body shape appears more compact and purposeful, although some see the new grille as an unnecessary intrusion.

The specification says it all. The GTV appeared on the market with the same two engines as originally offered on the GT. The 2.0-litre JTS petrol engine with a combination of lean-burn combustion system up to 1,500rpm, switching to stoichiometric (peak-efficiency) combustion at higher speeds, to deliver a crisp 82bhp per litre, 0–60mph in 8.4 seconds and a top speed of 137mph (220kph), sounds interesting enough. But with the car fitted with the full all-alloy, 24-valve, 3.2-litre V6 it shares with the 156 GTA and its more compact 147 stablemate, the performance increases to 240bhp and a 0–60 time of 6.3 seconds, and allows a top speed of 158mph (255kph). According to the company, this makes it the fastest production Alfa Romeo of all time.

Of course, straight-line performance isn't everything in real-world conditions. But to be fair to Alfa, they have done a great deal to provide the car with the right kind of responses. The McPherson strut front suspension now has a new front stabiliser bar to hold more of the power delivered by the big V6 down on to the road where it belongs. This is backed up by an

ABS braking system working through big ventilated discs front and rear, reinforced by an Electronic Brakeforce Distributor, and what Alfa describe as a 'sophisticated' Anti-Slip Regulation system.

Perhaps, in the end, the GTV – and the comparable Spider with its almost identical specification and its close family resemblance – represent the clearest evidence that the heart of the old company still beats on in full vigour within Alfa's adopted Fiat clothing. These cars look good, drive well, and are surprisingly economically priced for such an enticing combination of looks and performance. Unfortunately, it remains true that a pair of less welcome characteristics of the old days have survived the transition to new ownership and new standards of engineering. Alfa Romeo were always outstanding for doing what they did as well as they did while being almost permanently strapped for cash. Now it appears that producing cars in today's demanding and rapaciously competitive markets has become such an uncertain and fiendishly expensive business that even a company with pockets as deep as Fiat's is admitting to cash problems.

The other problem is more one of perception. In a recent programme made by BBC's *Top Gear* the latest version of the Alfa 166 was praised as a high quality and truly desirable car, an assessment which would normally bring the widest of smiles to the company board. But the report also revealed that the 166 could well lose just over half its value after its first year of ownership. At one time, the tumbling resale value of an Alfa reflected poor build quality, indifferent metallurgy, and rustproofing designed purely for the Italian climate. In a world where all these limitations have been addressed and eliminated, it seems hardly fair that Alfa residual values continue to slump so quickly. But this

problem relates to public perceptions and these are infinitely harder to change than solving engineering problems. Once Alfa can solve *that* particular problem, the new century could prove to be far more successful for the company, its cars, and their buyers, than the last one ever managed to be.

Opinions on the aesthetics of the GT among enthusiasts are divided – some find the front-end styling unsubtle and over elaborate – others approve of the bold statement of its enduring Alfa parentage. There is less controversy over the rear of the car, which is likely to be the view most familiar to those driving other marques.

Acknowledgements

There are many people I would like to thank for the help they gave in the preparation of this book, and they include:

Peter Marshall of the Alfa Romeo 1900 Register for kindly lending photos, and clarifying some points of information on the 1900s.

Chris Robinson of London-based Alfa specialist RM Restorations Ltd for generously spending much time discussing the strengths and the vulnerabilities of aged Alfas.

Chris Slade of the Alfa Romeo Owners' Club Montreal Register for his insights into owning and uprating the Montreal.

Tom Shrubb of BLS Automotive for guidance on the purchase and running of Alfasuds.

Les Dufty of Automeo for his detailed advice on the Alfetta family of 'transaxle' Alfas.

Mick Walsh, Richard Heseltine and Mark Hughes of 'Classic & Sports Car' magazine for sharing their experiences behind the wheel of the many Alfas they have driven over the years.

Elvira Ruocco of Alfa Romeo's archives in Italy, for the speedy provision of many superb photos.

Alwyn Kershaw of Malton, North Yorkshire, mechanical engineer and an Alfa dealer from 1965–1990, for invaluable advice on possible weaknesses of older model survivors.

Arnault Duprez of ANFIA in Turin, for help with production statistics.

The car on the front cover was photographed courtesy of Roberto Giordanelli.

Index